THE
HYDERABADIS

understanding of how great cities are shaped and reshaped in South Asia and how India's syncretic culture is preserved despite wounds of politics and history.'

—Mujibur Rehman

'This fascinating montage of Hyderabad and its ethos testifies to the pluralistic culture of a city that faces existential challenges in the twenty-first century. Majid's painstaking collation of oral histories weaves together glimpses of a fading civilization. This important book reminds us that Hyderabad's story is not that of a city but that of a subcontinent bruised by colonial past and majoritarianism of the present.'

—Raza Rumi

'Despite the dramatic lifestyle changes, colonization by dominant cultures, being sidelined in the administration and left to fend for themselves, [the Hyderabadis] faced their plight with bravery and stoic acceptance. Using personal narratives, including brief glimpses into his own family's experience and his journey while writing the book, Daneesh Majid beautifully covers historical context, cultural evolution, economic migration and political movements to provide a nuanced understanding of Hyderabad's history, culture and socio-political landscape from the time of India's independence to the present day.'

—Saaz Aggarwal

'Majid captures the essence and history of this unique city through the stories of its people. This book is a fascinating piece of oral history as well as an insightful account of contemporary lives in Hyderabad, a city that is at once of the past and the future.'

—Veenu Venugopal

THE HYDERABADIS

FROM 1947 TO THE PRESENT DAY

DANEESH MAJID

HarperCollins *Publishers* India

First published in India by HarperCollins *Publishers* 2025
HarperCollins *Publishers* India, Cyber City, Building 10-A,
Gurugram, Haryana-122002, India
www.harpercollins.co.in

2 4 6 8 10 9 7 5 3 1

Copyright © Daneesh Majid 2025

P-ISBN: 9789362135438
E-ISBN: 9789362134936

Typeset in 11/15 Minion Pro
by HarperCollins *Publishers* India Pvt. Ltd

Printed and bound at
Thomson Press (India) Ltd

HarperCollins *Publishers*, Macken House, 39/40 Mayor Street Upper,
Dublin 1, D01 C9W8, Ireland

شیراز بہار گلِ تر بکھر گیا

اب کس کو بتائیں کہ زیبِ چمن ہے کون

کشمیر میں کوئی تو کراچی میں ہے کوئی

اے زور کس سے پوچئے اہلِ دکن ہیں کون

۔ محی الدین قادری زور

Sheeraz bahaar gul-e-tar bikhar gaya
Ab kis ko bataayein ki zeb-e-chaman hai kaun
Kashmir mein koi to Karachi mein hai koi
Ay Zor kis se poochiye ehl-e-Deccan hai kaun

—Mohiuddin Qadri Zor

The detailed notes pertaining to this book are available on the HarperCollins *Publishers* India website. Scan this QR code to access the same.

Contents

Author's Note

This book would not have been possible without the willingness and accessibility of various families as well as individuals from different walks of life. For almost four years, they were my gateways into the past, present and future of Hyderabad. Some of them who were not Deccan natives were fortunate enough to be mentored and taught by two of the city's Urdu luminaries.

Five of these people—Halima Bi, Farooq Nazki, Zaheeruddin Ali Khan, Sampathamma Rao and Narayan Raj Saxena—are no longer with us.

This book is for them as well as my maternal grandmother, Meher Rahim, and late paternal uncle, Mohammed Abdul Qadeer. The former's father commissioned the construction of many mosques and temples as a high-ranking director in the Umoor-e-Mazhabi (Religious Affairs) Department during the Nizam's time. The latter was a part of the wave of Hyderabadis who went to Saudi Arabia to make a living for themselves in the 1980s.

Foreword

Buffeted by Time: Hyderabad in the Twenty-First Century

THE HYDERABAD I grew up in may have struck the outsider as provincial. For one, it was spatially compact. Abids was the glittering city centre, to be visited on special occasions. Mir Alam Mandi was a veritable cornucopia of fresh produce and exotic spices. The dawasaaz shops of Purani Haveli were the bases of apothecaries who occasionally doubled up as physicians, diagnosing as they dispensed. Anyone who needed anything printed came to the tightly clustered group of print shops in Chhatta Bazar. The automobile dealers of Osman Ganj, the bangle sellers of Lad Bazaar, even the hooch joints of Dhoolpet—there appeared to be tightly knit networks of commercial communities that made up hubs of economic activity. Residential areas acquired their own economic character. The uber-rich had begun moving to Banjara Hills, while middle-class enclaves like Himayat Nagar and Vijaynagar Colony were preferred by the office-going class. Festivals were defined by their rituals, many of them non-religious. Kite-flying on Makar Sankranti, dessert-consumption on Eid. The city had a rhythm that was distinctly different from the bustle of Bombay, the sarkari stuffiness of New Delhi, the orderliness of Madras and the chaos of Calcutta.

Scratch the provincial façade of Hyderabad however, and a palimpsest of a cosmopolis emerges. What was an Arab community doing in Barkas? How did the Kayasthas and Bilgramis of north India migrate here? Why did Hyderabad have an Iranian consulate even though it was not a national capital? Did it have anything to do with those famous cafes? The Marwaris from Rajasthan, the agriculturists-turned-industrialists from Andhra, the refugees of sectarian violence from Marathwada and the Indori migrants from Madhya Pradesh—all of them had found a seamless welcome in this city, enriching its culture. Daagh Dehlvi was buried here, as was Monsieur Raymond, a French adventurer whose grave was named 'Moosarambagh'. This was the city where James Achilles Kirkpatrick had romanced Khair-un-Nissa Begum, where the ethereal Turkish beauties Niloufer and Durr-e-Shehwar had reigned as princesses.

Nestled in the history of harmonious life were the scars of violent pasts and presents. The elders spoke of the 'Police Action' in hushed tones, and the folklore of many families—including mine—was replete with trauma from that genocidal week in September 1948. Periodic communal bloodletting in the form of 'riots' punctured the aura of inter-religious coexistence. The degradation of urban inequality was visible in the open drains of Dabirpura and Yaqutpura, contrasting against the wide avenues of Raj Bhavan and Begumpet. But overall, the atmosphere of Hyderabad veered towards the middle. We were more peaceful than violent, more tolerant than xenophobic, and more economically equal than unequal. *Ye bajaa, zeest pa-piyaada thi; dhoop se phir bhi chhaaon zyaada thi.* Even if we walked barefooted through life, there was more shade than sun.

One aspect of Hyderabad that made me especially proud was its revolutionary ethos. This was the city from where Turrebaz 'Turram'

Khan had launched an improbable and quixotic attack against the British. Makhdoom Mohiuddin and his fellow communists had cobbled together the Telangana Rebellion against the feudal nawabs and doras that had perfected their exploitative regimes under the Nizam's government. George Reddy had commenced his student agitation from Osmania University, sacrificing his life and inspiring generations of college students to remain socially active. In later years, activists like K.G. Kannabiran, Kandala Balagopal and the recently deceased G.N. Saibaba had enriched Hyderabad through their radical humanism. *Viplavaala yugam manade, viplaviste jayam manade*. The era of revolutions is ours, and if we revolutionize, victory is ours. The slogans that animated my Hyderabad had a cadence all their own.

Existing under the shadow of this revolutionary fervour was the underbelly of communalism. The sectarian divide between Hindus and Muslims in Hyderabad was simultaneously an inconvenient truth and an aberration. Despite the often-invoked harmony of the city, one had to contend with the reality of periodic violence between the communities, especially in the 1980s, after the infamous Ramiza Bi riots of 1978. The violence of the riots often left unfortunate demographic shifts in its aftermath. Over the past five decades, certain neighbourhoods became religiously concentrated, exacerbating the suspicion between the communities. Election speeches were often tinged with religious sloganeering and taunting. However, it would be safe to say that this divide still existed on the fringes. One would be hard-pressed to find a Hindu who did not have at least ten close Muslim friends and vice versa.

The Hyderabad of 2025, however, is a different space.

Global capitalism breached the walls of the idyll in the 1990s, bringing in the heady promise of 'Cyberabad' and setting the city on a breathless rollercoaster. The influx of capital into the city acquired a critical mass, producing raging boom-and-bust cycles in real estate and increasing inequality coefficients. There are buildings with fancy names like 'Mindspace IT Park' and 'Cyber Pearl', which host an alphabet soup of multinational corporations. The managers of those firms prefer to live in twenty-plus-storied residential fortresses, where the domestic staff is screened twice by security phalanxes through phone apps.

As an axiomatic side effect, the trajectories of development in the city have become vastly more uneven. The drains in Yaqutpura remain open, while the new-rich, having saturated Jubilee Hills, produce gilded enclaves in erstwhile villages with quaint names like Shaikpet and Kokapet. The malls of Madhapur charge ten times for the same dresses as those in the shops of Sultan Bazaar and get away with it. Inequalities are not restricted to the economic zone, but also produce cultural separation. The discourse of religious binaries has become more fractious, and the uniquely shared sacred spaces that had characterized the Hyderabad of yore have begun to shrink.

The older denizens have looked on with bemusement as the geographic and symbolic loci of the city shift. Is it the city's destiny to lose its contiguities and emerge as a cultural archipelago? Change is, of course, the axiomatic condition of life, but my generation could be excused for feeling wistful due to all the rapid transformations taking place. A city that had developed a unique character over four centuries was being flattened and homogenized by the battering rams of capitalism. As someone who grew up in the Old City and still calls it home, I am acutely aware of how ineffectual my hand-wringing might seem to a young person. I knew that my sentiments, antiquated as they may seem, had an ineffable authenticity to them, and I hankered to communicate them with members of a new generation.

It was thus a pleasure when I made the acquaintance of Daneesh Majid five years ago. A young man who came of age in the new millennium, Daneesh possessed an understanding about the psyche of the city, which bordered on the prescient, without being anachronistic. His knowledge of the cityscape of Hyderabad was granular in the extreme. He knew where the second-hand booksellers dwelt. He could speak eloquently about the literary legacy of the Bachelors' Quarters near Moazam Jahi Market. He had interviewed the shroud merchants of Old City about their role in the political economy of Muslim funerals. He could identify the leftist poets of the city who had made a mark on the democratic traditions of India. And in a delightful nod to his generation, he shed light on the growing popularity of mixed martial arts in the Old City.

During my conversations with Daneesh, I learned that he was planning a book on Hyderabad. In time, I read its draft and was most gratified by its structure, a series of bio-sketches of luminaries whose lives mostly traversed the second half of the twentieth century. Despite my pretences of being a history-keeper of the city, I learned much from these pages that I had not known. This book is neither a historical record of the city nor an exhaustive account of the lives of the personages it profiles. Rather, like a slide projector of yore, it provides glimpses of different facets of Hyderabadi history, evoking nostalgia or curiosity, depending on one's level of familiarity with the city.

Reading this book, I had a gratifying epiphany. The ethos of Hyderabad that I remember may have faded into the background, but it has not disappeared. Indeed, not only does it remain rooted in its citizens, it has also diffused across the world through its diaspora. We might be right in expressing concern at how a sense of Hyderabadi-ness is fading, but in its own way, it is in no danger of disappearing. Every time the traditions of plurality are threatened, old histories of Hyderabad re-emerge to restore equanimity. Every time someone tries to tear apart its 'Isa-Moosi tehzeeb', a new generation of Hyderabadis like Daneesh will emerge to claw back a shared space of Hyderabadi-ness. And so we will beat on, against the currents of

McDonaldization while also avoiding the eddies of empty nostalgia. To quote the great Josh Malihabadi:

> *Waqt ka farman apna rukh badal sakta nahin*
> *Maut tal sakti hai ab farman tal sakta nahin*

> The decree of time may change its course to catch its breath
> But the verdict of that time is even more unyielding than death

Raza Mir
Professor, William Paterson University,
and author

Prologue

IT ALL STARTED with a piece of work that fell short of a chief editor's expectations. Mir Ayoob Ali Khan, my boss at Siasat.com, had asked me to interview a few Hyderabadis who had worked in the Persian Gulf and had now returned to the city in their middle age.

One of them was Arshad Pirzada.

The first cut of the video interview with Pirzada could not have been more disappointing for Khan. He chided me for only reciting a laundry list of Pirzada's achievements. There were many, chief among them being the school he had opened in the Toli Chowki area for children from low-income families. But Khan, a childhood friend of Pirzada's, wanted the interview to also highlight his many struggles.

I was not the only one pulled up. Pirzada, too, was given an earful by Khan for underplaying the exalted status his family occupied during the Nizam's reign and the dire straits they were plunged into after Police Action.

In a way, the dramatic arc of Pirzada's life represented the trajectories of Hyderabad's many Muslim families—both aristocratic and non-aristocratic alike. That is the flavour the editor wanted captured.

Pirzada's lineage was a storied one. His maternal grandfather had been a high-level secretary in the Peshi department, which dealt with the affairs of Hyderabad's sprawling royal family. He, like most of the Nizam's subjects, had not foreseen the ignominious end to the 224-year-old Asaf Jahi empire in 1948.

The run-up and aftermath to the integration of Hyderabad into the newly independent India had precipitated a saga of blood and violence that might have received a lot more attention if it were not for larger scale tragedies (Partition) and existential threats (the Kashmir war of 1947–48) unfolding in the northern parts of the country. In Hyderabad, even the Indian military's brisk takeover was given the more innocuous-sounding name of 'Police Action'.

Families like Pirzada's had no place in the new dispensation. Overnight, the language of the administration changed from Urdu to English. A lot of the old elite was sidelined, both politically and economically. And that was why Pirzada and many other Muslims left the comforts of their homes and set off for a country where their pre-1948 privilege would mean nothing.

During the 1970s, Gulf countries like Saudi Arabia paved the road on which Hyderabad's Muslims would find their feet. By working his way up from store assistant to counter salesman and then heading a branch of a Riyadh-based automotive company, Pirzada was able to put his children through school, build a new house for his family and ultimately become a benefactor for his community.

A Silently Successful Minority

What surprised Khan about my failure to produce a lively draft was the fact that my own family's trajectory had not been too different from Pirzada's. I was a direct beneficiary of the post-1948 Hyderabadi Muslim renaissance in the Gulf, as my father worked a white-collar job with Saudi Airlines for a long time. Khan, who had his own Saudi connection (Chapter 5), was keen for more of these ordinary stories to be told, particularly in a climate that is communally charged. 'We were left to fend for ourselves after 1948,' Khan told me on that afternoon in February 2020. 'By working hard, we bounced back. Now the powers that be want to inflict a similar 1948-like calamity to undo what we have accomplished.'

Khan's words ended up crystallizing something that I had been vaguely thinking about for some time. That conversation made me realize that the vicissitudes of ordinary Hyderabadis do not figure heavily in narratives about the Police Action and its aftermath. Whatever stories I had read and heard were about the Nizam and the reign of terror unleashed by the Razakars who cherished the doomed dream of Hyderabad's independence. There was little attention paid to the fallout on the lives of the Nizam's subjects, the kind of people who lent the erstwhile princely state of Hyderabad its distinct character.

Hyderabad's Muslims cannot be boxed into the caricatures showcased though pop culture, media or India's many film industries.[1] One stereotype is the cultured, fluent Urdu-speaker who usually comes from landed lineage. There are others, too: the bearded gangster, puncture-wallah the militant extremist, the skullcap-wearing ghetto-dweller.

There is also a difference in the trajectories of the Muslim community in the north and south of the country. I grew up abroad, but on my visits to Hyderabad, I had always seen Muslims with and without visible markers of identity shopping for nice clothes, eating at upscale restaurants and enrolling their children in top educational institutions. The situation was different in the north—the average Muslim had not been as integrated into the upper middle class or middle class in the way that Hyderabad's largest minority seemed to mesh into those strata.[2]

Yet, in mainstream discourse, we do not hear as many stories about the fall-and-rise of Hyderabad's Muslims. However, as I went about understanding and collecting these stories, many inconvenient realties also emerged. I also realized that I need not restrict myself to stories of Hyderabadi Muslims, who formed 15 per cent of the total population at the time of integration. To paint a more complete portrait, I would have to also delve deep into the stories of Kayasthas and Telugu-speaking Hindus.

Learning and Unlearning

The Asaf Jahi Nizam's territory consisted of present-day Telangana, the northeastern part of Karnataka and Maharashtra's Marathwada region. Growing up, many of my elders would tell me how life in the princely state resembled what one would imagine life to be in a sovereign paradise. Hyderabad had its own postal system, luxury cars and many other privileges that were unheard of in British India. Many Muslims tend to view the Nizam's rule through rose-tinted glasses. After I understood the concept of the British Empire hovering over the Nizams via paramountcy, the 'sovereign' part of that immaculate conception was put to rest.

From the early 1700s until 1948, a Muslim minority reigned over the Hindu majority. With the Mughals consolidating the Deccan kingdoms through military action by 1687, Urdu and Persian sidelined local languages, including Dakhani Urdu.

Writing about Hyderabad for different publications and reading accounts of princely Hyderabad attuned me to another truth that many of my family members and Hyderabadis had chosen to downplay. While the city owes a lot to the seventh Nizam who famously said that Hindus and Muslims are his two eyes, I learned that the pre-1948 ruling dispensation was not entirely benign for the majority of Osman Ali Khan's population. And with the state being home to different political ideologies and aspirations that cut through religious, ethnic and linguistic lines, not every Telanganite remembers Police Action as completely tragic.

In my formative years, I had a sense that there were groups of people that certain elite Muslims did not consider 'true Hyderabadis'. People who would fall into this category included those who did not hail from Hyderabad city and those who did not speak the more urban Dakhani.

To develop a more balanced, non-utopian view of the old days, I credit my many conversations with Telugu-speakers. Those who did not hold this peachy view of princely Hyderabad spoke to me about the feudal oppression and bonded labour that was rampant in the Nizam's dominions. They led me to literature about the Telangana Peasants' Rebellion, which was more focused on the cleavages in class rather than religion. I came to see that the red rebellion of the youth against the landed gentry may not have been mediated by saffron or green.

As I went farther back in my reading of Hyderabad's history, I arrived at answers to some contemporary questions. The Qutub Shahi emperors—who preceded the Nizams—had overseen a state where linguistic and religious traditions had converged. Back then, Telugu had the same status as Persian and Urdu.[3] Dakhani was born in the pre-Asaf Jahi era, as Urdu mingled with the Marathi and Kannada that was spoken in the surrounding sultanates.

Muslim Rulers, Hindu Subjects

It also became clear to me that solely presenting Hyderabad as some sort of syncretic paradise was a fool's endeavour. There have always been fault lines between the religions, and there have always been factions who seek to exploit them. In the 1930s and '40s, it was the Majlis Ittehad-ul-Muslimeen (MIM), its voluntary militant wing known as the Razakars, the Arya Samaj, the Hindu Mahasabha and certain elements within the Hyderabad State Congress (HSC).

Eventually, it was a religious ideologue whose impossible dream led the princely state to its denouement. He encouraged the Nizam's quixotic desire for independence. His militia, the Razakars, ran riot over the countryside, threatening and torturing those who opposed the vision of an independent Hyderabad. The Indian government played ball for a while—Nehru even promised 40 per cent Muslim representation in the new government[4]—until it could do it no more. The Nizam's unwillingness to go quietly forced the government's hand and put it on a collision course with a paltry army of 24,000 soldiers led by General Ahmed El-Edroos.

Due to the Razakars' excesses, the Hindu population of the city too had been alienated. There were other enablers. While Delhi was preoccupied by the war in Kashmir, Hyderabad's Foreign Minister Moin Nawaz Jung had taken the issue to the Security Council;[5] Australian gun-runner Sydney Cotton was smuggling weapons in. But the tipping point was yet to come. After the pro-Congress Urdu journalist Shoaibullah Khan was murdered, the military marched into Hyderabad. It took five days to mop the whole affair up.

What followed before and after the annexation was one of independent India's closely guarded secrets. According to the recently declassified Pandit Sunderlal Committee Report, 30,000–40,000 Muslims were massacred—sometimes on the mere claim that they were Razakars.[6] At the time, Home Minister Sardar Patel dismissed these reports as 'lacking balance and proportion'.[7]

One of those people who narrowly escaped death was my paternal grandfather. When posted as a doctor in the Nizam's army in Aurangabad, the Indian military attacked his camp. The camp's soldiers and personnel were lined up and shot. Somehow, the barrage of bullets missed him.

Appropriating History

Each of the ten chapters in this book has a protagonist. What helped me zero in on them was my objective to address three misconceptions about Police Action: (a) that only Hindus suffered in Asaf Jahi Hyderabad; (b) that Muslims had no role whatsoever in deposing an establishment ruled by their 'own'; (c) only the Congress spearheaded the anti-Nizam struggle.

Today, the powers that be continue to rake up this schism of past atrocities to polarize Telangana on religious lines. During the 2023 Telangana Legislative Assembly campaigns, then Chief Minister Kalvakuntla Chandrashekar Rao and his party were labelled 'modern Razakars,'[8] thereby likening them to the oppressive Muslim rulers who stood tall over the majority Hindu population.

With the anti-Nizam campaign being seen through a religious prism, a conversation about the Telangana Peasants' Rebellion with teacher-turned-politician Chukka Ramaiah (Chapter 7) brought to light how even Muslims were negatively affected by the exploitative feudal setup. Unfortunately, the communist strand of the anti-feudal struggle finds little prominence in the discourse around Police Action.

In his memoir, Puchalapalli Sundarayya, the communist leader from the Madras Presidency, mentioned that India's military action had a second component to it. With the Razakars and other anti-accession forces quelled, the army had its sights on clamping down on the Telangana Peasants' Rebellion.[9]

An Overlooked Part of the Past

Similarly, the long struggle for a separate Telangana state has its origins in an often-missing thread of the story of Hyderabad's accession to the Indian Union. The population within Hyderabad state's Telugu-speaking districts welcomed the ouster of the Asaf Jahi establishment. Yet, even after the Police Action, which saw many Muslim casualties in the Marathi- and Kannada-speaking regions of the princely state, a certain section of the Left and the Indian government were at loggerheads. The neighbouring Andhra communists, who shared a language with Telangana's Telugu population, helped them in their struggle against the princely state's feudal dispensation.

With New Delhi weary of the growing communist influence in Hyderabad's Mahabubnagar, Warangal and Nalgonda districts, and the leftists viewing the Indian government as an oppressive bourgeoise democracy, the battle raged on. Andhraites like Sundarayya toed the China line that wanted the armed struggle to continue. Some prominent leftists like the late Burgula Narsing Rao even saw this as an early fissure of the Andhra–Telangana divide that was to play out later.[10] People like Chukka Ramaiah (Chapter 7) and Apparasu Srinivasa Rao (Chapter 8) helped me understand these dynamics.

While there were many Telugu-speaking subjects of the Hyderabad state who were happy to become a part of Andhra Pradesh, several also harboured apprehensions about the influx of what they saw as 'outsiders' in Telangana. Burgula Ramakrishna Rao, the second and last chief minister of Hyderabad, portended the concerns about Andhra hegemony in a letter to then Indian National Congress President U.N. Dhebar.[11] He spoke about the 'harsh' and 'unrelenting' treatment meted out by Andhra officers to a debilitated population that was still reeling from the Razakars' campaign of terror.

The Mulki Question and Telangana's Telugus

The insider–outsider debate was not new to the Deccan. During the Bahmani and Qutub Shahi eras, the indigenous 'Deccanis' and 'Afaqi' Persians from other parts of the Islamic world were always at odds.[12] During the fourth Nizam's reign, Prime Minister Salar Jung brought in many learned Hindus—particularly Kayasthas—and north Indian Muslims to fill key bureaucratic as well as academic posts.

Much before a similar movement in Maharashtra, a son-of-the-soil sentiment had gripped a united Hyderabad in 1952 with the Madras Presidency's Telugus already being implanted in former Asaf Jahi domains. Post-accession, the first iteration of the Mulki versus non-Mulki situation surfaced through a student agitation against those not indigenous to the deposed Nizam's dominions. The fact that non-Mulkis occupied key positions in academia and administration was the cause of a lot of discontent.[13] These demonstrations began in Warangal, about 150 kilometres northeast of Hyderabad city. Slogans like 'Non-Mulkis go back', '*Idli-sambar ghar ko jaao* (Idli-sambar go home)' and 'Students' Union Zindabad' began reverberating across the state.[14] Only after the death of Potti Sriramulu who wanted a separate state for Madras Presidency's Telugus, did the Andhra state come into existence with Kurnool as its capital in 1953.

The states' reorganization in 1956 meant that the Marathi- and Kannada-speaking parts of the erstwhile Nizam's dominions went to Maharashtra and Karnataka respectively. Telangana was merged with the Telugu-speaking regions that were once a part of the Madras Presidency to form the state of Andhra Pradesh. Hyderabad became its capital city. But the insider–outsider agitation continued.

In 1960, it centred around the Kothagudem Thermal Power Plant, where only 200 of the 1,400 employees were from Telangana.[15] After eight years, 175 of them had been retrenched. In protest, many of these workers fasted and also shouted slogans like 'Non-Mulkis go back!' More protests were to follow with the non-gazetted officials rising up to demand more safeguards for jobs before the first push for statehood that saw 369 people killed. On a political level, the Telangana Praja Samithi (TPS)—the precursor to the Telangana Rashtra Samithi and later the Bharat Rashtra Samithi—took up the cause of the struggle. But the party was dissolved as President Marri Chenna Reddy came to an understanding with Indira Gandhi to call off the campaign.

But the grievances continued to pile up. The one-sided distribution of resources was compounded by a sharper awareness of the distinct culture of Telangana.

For instance, Hyderabadi cuisine like shaami (patties made out of meat and lentils), paya (soup stew with goat trotters) or khichdi-khatta (flavoured rice with sour, thick gravy) can be found on the tables of both Hindu and Muslim households of Telangana. The Telangana and Dakhani dialects deviate from the more conventional versions of Telugu and Urdu respectively. This composite culture was perhaps best embodied by the Kayasthas of Hyderabad, who had long served as administrators for the Nizams.

From Nizam to Revanth Reddy: The Trajectory of the Kayasthas

That brought me to another integral strand of the story. A book titled *The Hyderabadis* would be incomplete without looking at the evolution of this influential community. The Kayasthas' impact on the city's fortunes cannot be understated. A non-Telanganite witnessing a conversation between someone with a last name like Saxena, Mathur or Srivastava and me will probably have a hard time determining who is Hindu and who is Muslim. The old adage of Kayasthas being aadhe Musalman[16]—half Muslim—is for good reason.

As powerful bureaucrats, administrators and learned academics within Asaf Jahi Hyderabad, they were indispensable to the Nizams. Kayasthas like Raj Bahadur Gour (Chapter 9), who participated in the Telangana Rebellion, and his cousin Oudesh Rani Bawa are still seen as embodiments of the composite culture of Hyderabad that has roots in medieval India.

Kayasthas, too, have seen their identities evolve from the pre-Mughal periods to more contemporary times. As late as the early twentieth century, having Muslim wives alongside Kayastha ones was the practice among elites of both communities in the Asaf Jahi state.

Any discussion about the past, present and future of Hyderabad and Telangana would be incomplete without this cosmopolitan community. Like Muslims, they have also had to adapt to the vagaries of time.

Beyond Nehru, the Nizam, Patel, Razvi and Munshi

One of the main reasons I conceived this project was to memorialize the constants and changes in Hyderabadi society. My conception of Hyderabad was wide from the beginning—the 'Hyderabadis' within the book's title refers not just to denizens of Hyderabad city, but people who have family connections to the areas that were encompassed by the erstwhile princely state of Hyderabad. For obvious reasons, the Muhammad Quli Qutub Shah-founded city plays a central role in the narrative—so many stories end up unfolding in the capital of Telangana.

Even before this project got its green light, I started interviewing people across different generations, acquiring oral histories, reading Urdu and English literature and gathering my own family's experiences. I started by speaking to families whose members had lived through the following events: the 1948 Police Action, the Telangana Peasants' Rebellion that took place from the mid-1930s to the early '50s, the 1956 linguistic division that resulted in the Telangana region of the erstwhile princely state becoming a part of Andhra Pradesh, the numerous phases of the Telangana Agitation since 1969 and the formation of the state in 2014. I have also tried to understand what this means in the vitiated atmosphere of post-2014 India.

There is a corpus of literature available on the tumultuous period during, before and after Hyderabad's merger. These works include *The Destruction of Hyderabad* by A.G. Noorani, *The Tragedy of Hyderabad* by Mir Laiq Ali, *Police Action: A Misnomer* by Pandu Ranga Reddy and *Hyderabad 1948: An Avoidable Invasion* by Syed Ali Hashmi. Srinath Raghavan's book *War and Peace in Modern Asia* features a case study on the event from a security standpoint. Mohammed Hyder's book *October Coup* is a memoir told from the point of view of the former Osmanabad (in present-day Maharashtra) district collector. John Zubrzycki's *The Last Nizam* has a chapter on the accession to Hyderabad before he focuses on the titular eighth Nizam Mukarram Jah.

Most accounts on Hyderabad have come 'from above', so to speak. Ordinary people appear as mere pawns in the grand games played by powerful men. Events appear as milestones that turn the political tide, while their consequences on citizens are ignored or flattened in sweeping generalizations. I wanted to go against this grain. I wanted to use the same framing device of events to zoom in on the lives and times of the people who participated and lived through them.

The ten chapters in this book shed light on how different families navigated interesting times from Police Action to the present day. Some were a part of the aristocratic stock or close to those segments of society.

Many, such as *Siasat* co-founder Abid Ali Khan (Chapter 1), Chukka Ramaiah, Apparasu Sheshagiri Rao (Chapter 8) and Raj Bahadur Gour, even took to the onset of Marxism that found numerous adherents among youth throughout the princely state.

Not many know that Pakistan was an early outpost for Hyderabadis after Police Action. My paternal grandfather Mohammed Abdul Ghaffar (Chapter 3) came close to being a part of the post-1948 Muslim exodus from Hyderabad state as well. Unlike the now Canada-based Hyderabadi–Pakistani Ali Adil Khan's father (Chapter 6), Dr Ghaffar ended up staying back. His son, my father, would instead undertake a long but temporary migration to Saudi Arabia as an expatriate.

Urdu luminaries like Mohiuddin Qadri Zor and Abdul Qadir Sarwari (Chapter 4) also left their hometowns, but not for another country. To ply their trade in a place where there would be patronage for it, they made Srinagar in Jammu and Kashmir their home.

When speaking to Narayan Raj Saxena (Chapter 10) and former Jamaat-e-Islami student wing member Umar Faruq Quadri (Chapter 2), I came to understand how fluid people's identities can be due to economic and broader political circumstances.

This journey of chronicling their lives was not just historical and political. In fact, it became more personal as I got to further rediscover my roots and hometown. While I was researching this book, the same past that I was discovering to contain multitudes was being painted in monochromatic tones by politicians and a section of the media. Inconvenient truths were being brushed under the carpet because they came in the way of narratives neatly folding over themselves. But Hyderabad cannot be bottled so easily.

If one ventures through the length and breadth of the city, they will find landmarks that prove this. The Arts and Commerce College building of Osmania University, which blends Hindu, Indo-Saracenic and Qutub Shahi architecture is on display for all to see.[17] About 10 kilometres south of Osmania University is the Charminar. It stands as a symbol of not just Hyderabad but the Qutub Shahi monarch who ordered its construction. Quli Qutub Shah and other rulers of his family infused Hyderabad with a pluralistic ethos that survives against all odds. It is no surprise, that in honour of the city which the Golconda monarch founded, he wrote, fittingly, in Dakhani:

Mera shehr logaan se maamur kar
Rakhiya joon toon dariya mein min ya sami

Fill up my city with people,
My God, just as you have filled the river with fish

Abid Ali Khan: A Rebel among His Own

سلطانی جمہور کا آتا ہے زمانہ

جو نقشِ کہن تم کو نظر آئے مٹا دو

—علامہ اقبال

Sultani jamhoor ka aata hai zamana
Jo naqsh-e-kuhan tum ko nazar aaye mita do

The rule of the princely kingdom approaches its end
Remove and annihilate every imprint of the old guard

—Allama Iqbal

IN THE EARLY 1930s, a prominent noble, Mir Mehmood Ali Khan, received a letter from Osman Ali Khan. To Mehmood, Osman was a former classmate. To the population of Hyderabad, the largest princely state in British India, Osman Ali Khan was 'Alaa Hazrat', His Exalted Highness. He was princely Hyderabad's seventh Nizam, the latest in the Asaf Jahi line that ruled a vast territory of a little over 2,00,000 square kilometres.

The Nizam was writing to his old friend to warn him about the company his son was keeping at Osmania University (OU). 'He is veering away from his aristocratic roots with the leftist circles that are growing day by day in Osmania,' the Nizam wrote, 'Make sure he does not get led astray or he will become a communist.' The Nizam's spies had reported that Abid Ali Khan, Mehmood's son, had come under the influence of the Comrades' Association, a group of eclectic and socially conscious students. Founded by Alam Khundmiri, Syed Ibrahim, Qutub-e-Alam, Hassan Ali Meeraj, Manik Lal Gupta, S. Nagar Rao and N.K. Rao,[1] the group emerged as a counter to communal organizations that were either pro- or anti-Nizam. One was the Hindu-centric Arya Samaj, whose cadre would join the Hyderabad State Congress (HSC), while the other was the Majlis Ittehad-ul-Muslimeen (MIM), which sought to uphold Muslim rule.

In those days, Osmania was a hotbed of an uprising against the unjust feudal system that the university's namesake presided over. The Congress strand of the anti-Nizam movement began playing out with a satyagraha (non-violent political resistance), whose struggle found expression in OU through the slogan '*Vande Mataram*'. But a Marxist campaign had also been brewing at the university alongside the Congress one.

OU: A Growing Leftist Stronghold

The Bolsheviks' ouster of the Czarist regime in Russia had a ripple effect among students and youngsters in British India. Professors who had studied abroad or been exposed to literature from there were discussing communist ideas in the classroom. One such educator was Habib-ur-Rahman, an Aligarh Muslim University graduate from Hyderabad who had been sent to the London School of Economics (LSE) on a government scholarship.

Sajjad Shahid, historian and son of the leftist litterateurs Hussaini Shahid and Zeenat Sajida, told me that Rahman had come under the influence of Harold Laski at the LSE. Shahid elaborated, 'Like most of these Indian youngsters who gained exposure to such ideas, Rahman returned to India. He then started teaching at OU.'

Other Osmania teachers who had been exposed to Marxist ideas included religious and cultural studies professor Khalifa Abdul Hakim and English professor Hussain Ali Khan.

Though Abid Ali Khan was not a card-carrying member of the Comrades' Association and despite being from well-off families that shielded them from the gristly realities of everyday life, he and other college-going Hyderabadi students were now questioning their feudal privilege.

A Red Scare among the Blue-Blooded

Aiwan-e-Ghazal (The House of Ghazal) is a novel by Jeelani Bano. It is set in, around and after the Police Action. In it, Wahid Hussain, the patriarch of an aristocratic family, finds himself at odds with his son-in-law, Haidar Ali Khan, an England-educated lawyer and communist sympathizer.

When Haider visits Hussain's palatial home, his brother-in-law Rashid asks him, 'Dulha Bhai,[2] will your communists really snatch all our wealth away to distribute it among the poor, so that all the low-born will be elevated to the same status as us nawabs?'[3]

Haider responds caustically, 'Brace yourself up for many such injustices! It is quite possible that a field hand will rule over you after he wins the elections. Thus, leaving you wondering at the injustice of it all.'[4]

The response angers his father-in-law, who then warns, 'Haidar Pasha, be careful! CID officers have already submitted their reports on you to Ali Pasha. They say that your speeches regarding fascism and international politics are a smokescreen for your agenda against how things work around here. You are found at programmes organized by the Communist Party.'[5]

In the same vein, Abid's iconoclastic tendencies were clearly a cause for worry to his family. After all, his maternal grandfather, Intekhab Jung, and paternal grandfather, Saulat Jung, studied alongside Alaa-Hazrat's father and the sixth Nizam Mahbub Ali Khan, at Madrassa-e-Aliya.

The middle child among thirteen children, Abid did what he could to shun his privilege. As was common among colonial India's aristocracy, three of his brothers went to England to earn their bachelor's degrees. Motabar Ali Khan did accountancy, Khalilullah Khan studied commerce and Basheeruddin Khan pursued an engineering degree.

Not one to toe the line, Abid instead opted to enrol at OU. His English was excellent and would serve him well anywhere, but he decided to undertake his college education in his mother tongue.

Zaheeruddin Ali Khan, his nephew and adopted son, remembered, 'Despite being from a landed lineage, Abba (father) deviated heavily from the practices of the gentry. In the very exclusive stratum of Hyderabad, he used to treat a servant's kid like an equal.'

At college, Abid decided that he was not just going to live and interact with his own. Hostel A in Osmania exclusively housed noble and upper middle-class students. Students who came from less well-off families lived in Hostel C. Abid chose to stay in Hostel B, where he met a diverse, socially conscious group of comrades who would also cement their names in Hyderabad's leftist lore. These included people like Mir Hassan, Shahabuddin and the revolutionary poet and trade unionist Makhdoom Mohiuddin. Hostel C was also where he met Mehboob Hussain Jigar, with whom he would go on to establish the Urdu daily, *Roznama-e-Siasat*.

The Progressive Writers' Association

In the classroom, Abid diligently went about his studies in Philosophy, Political Science and Economics. But the Marxist influences around him attuned him to the world of progressive literature. He became founding secretary of the Hyderabad chapter of the Progressive Writers' Association (PWA), which had been established in Lucknow in 1936. In 1942, at the age of twenty-two, he translated Karl Marx's *Wage, Labour and Capital* into Urdu. Three years later, the PWA's conference was held in Hyderabad. As the convenor,[6] Abid was in the thick of building networks between Urdu writers from north India and the Deccan.[7]

By the time he graduated, he had married into a priestly family of the Shah Khamosh shrine located in the Dar-us-Salaam area. Mehmood Ali Khan hoped that marriage and a job as a translator within the Prime Minister's Department of Information would quell his son's rebellious tendencies.

But Abid had other plans. His work with the PWA had exposed him to socially conscious journalism. Along with his old hostel mate Jigar, who was now working in the Department of Customs, Abid had set his sights on launching a publication.

It was a period of great churn in Hyderabad. Many of their OU classmates who were in the Comrades' Association had officially joined the Communist Party of India; and the nationalist sympathizers had become card-carrying members of the Congress. Both these parties were ratcheting up the pressure to accede to the Indian Union.

Khan and Jigar knew that merger was the only way forward considering the princely state's Hindu-majority population and its geographic limitations as a landlocked territory. They were in favour of the socialist, democratic setup that was being talked about. But this new order would not surface until religious tensions engulfed British India.

A Tense Landscape

From the late 1800s and well into the early 1900s, religious organizations like the MIM and the Arya Samaj had taken a communal line. To hasten the accession, the Arya Samaj, Hindu Mahasabha and the paramilitary volunteer organization Rashtriya Swayamsevak Sangh (RSS) launched raids upon Marathi-speaking parts of Hyderabad—sometimes with the patronage of certain sections within the Hyderabad State Congress.

The MIM ran a military wing, whose volunteers were known as Razakars. After prominent Majlis figurehead Bahadur Yar Jung's death, the MIM now belonged to the rabble-rousing, firebrand Qasim Razvi. When it came to negotiations between the Indian government and Hyderabad, Razvi did whatever he could to prevent a positive breakthrough.

Jawaharlal Nehru, the first Prime Minister of independent India, had extended an olive branch to the Asaf Jahi establishment by offering 40 per cent of Muslim representation in the new democratic setup. That too, much to the dismay of Home Minister Sardar Vallabhbhai Patel.[8]

Muslims also dominated 70 per cent of the police, 55 per cent of the army and 26 per cent of the administration.[9] That olive branch was a good deal considering the fact that Muslims constituted a meagre 12 per cent of the princely state's population as per the 1941 census.

Under the prime ministership of the Nawab of Chhatari, Abid's employer, the Nizam and his council had approved a Standstill Agreement in October 1947 after negotiations with the Indian government.[10] Both sides even agreed that if Hyderabad agreed to merge with India, there would be ample scope to hash out finer details of the accession later.[11]

Had the delegation been allowed to fly to Delhi with this agreement where it was about to be signed, so many lives could have been saved.[12] But massive demonstrations organized by Qasim Razvi outside the homes of delegates, which included the Nawab of Chhatari, prevented them from going to the airport.

The MIM chief grew so powerful that he replaced the Nawab of Chhatari with a more pliable Prime Minister, Mir Laiq Ali. The bureaucracy and cabinet-level ministries were under Razvi's thumb.[13]

Meanwhile, the Razakars were running rampant on the ground. Between April 1947 and March 1948, the militia looted or set fire to 250 villages, burnt down 4,000 houses and assaulted 450 women throughout the state.[14]

Abid Ali Khan was watching these events unfold. His son Zaheer told me that he felt strongly about the Razakars' atrocities on Hindus being underreported by the administration's Department of Information, as well as the newspapers. He resigned from his job.

After resigning, Jigar and Abid became trainees at the Urdu newspaper *Payaam*. Launched in 1934 by Qazi Abdul Ghaffar, a former public information officer who became an important voice in Hyderabad's publication *Hum-Dard* as well as other Indian Urdu dailies, *Payaam*'s goal was to maintain communal harmony amidst the Hindu–Muslim discord that had taken shape in the state. Prominent progressive Akthar Hassan had taken over *Payaam* in the early 1940s, when financial and government pressures were wearing down the publication.[15]

In fact, it was the Razakars' brutal killing of a journalist that served as one of the final straws for sending the military into Hyderabad. Shoaibullah Khan, the pro-Congress editor of the Urdu newspaper *Imroz*, had been shot on 22 August 1948 by the Razakars.[16] The bullet in the back was not enough for the MIM militia. It also wanted to send a message to anybody who voiced any opposition to it by also chopping off Khan's hand.

After this, even the pacifist Nehru relented and accepted that the military needed to be sent to Hyderabad.

To Sajjad Shahid though, other than ousting the Asaf Jahis, India's military action had a second component to it. With the Razakars and other anti-accession forces quelled, the army had its sights on the task of clamping down upon the Peasants' Rebellion in Telangana.

While many of their university comrades like Raj Bahadur Gour (Chapter 9), Makhdoom Mohiuddin and Burgula Narsing Rao contributed to this struggle as CPI members, Abid and Jigar did not align themselves with a particular political faction.

With a new guard coming in after 1948, a sense of despondency set in among Muslims. They were sidelined in the military and civilian administration. English replaced Urdu as the government language. Government employees who did not have much of a grasp on English were asked to build their fluency in the language or resign. On top of that, Muslims did not have much of a presence in the business landscape.

Khan and Jigar ramped up their activism to try and bridge the widening trust deficit between the two communities. Dead cows lying in temples and pigs in mosques were common sights. The duo would often venture to these places of worship to get rid of the remains. The festering of these communal wounds convinced them that something needed to be done to stitch up the ruptures in Hyderabadi society.

A Bridge between Hyderabad's Muslims and an Independent India

'In their heart of hearts, Abba and Jigar Chacha wanted to start a newspaper, but many of their elders prodded them to open their own dairy farm,' revealed Zaheer Ali Khan.

Urdu-related endeavours were hard to come by for Muslims. It is one of the main reasons that many of them began thinking seriously about a future in Pakistan. Khan and Jigar made it their mission to foster communal harmony, promote the Urdu language, and encourage Hyderabadi Muslims to remain in India. With those goals in mind, their publication named *Siasat* was launched on 15 August 1949.

Despite being financially sound with land and certain assets, purchasing a printing press seemed to be a bad idea. Their well-wishers' advice of buying or investing in a dairy farm would have likely yielded quicker and better returns. However, Abid's mother was more than willing to help get her son's venture off the ground. She sold a lot of her jewellery and property to pay for the printing press.

Besides daily news, *Siasat* published the work of Hyderabad's left-leaning poets, humourists and intellectuals, many of whom Khan and Jigar knew from their Progressive Writers' Association days. Though to Khan and other like-minded individuals, a newspaper could only do so much.

To start afresh, Hyderabad state would have to be dismantled.

Meanwhile, the Telangana Peasants' Rebellion raged on in Hyderabad state's Nalgonda, Warangal and Mahabubnagar districts.

Telangana–Andhra Splinters

This struggle saw the Telangana and Andhra contingents first coming together under the banner of the Andhra Jana Sangham in the early 1920s. The Sangham was the predecessor to the Andhra Mahasabha, which would come to be closely associated with the Communist Party of India.

The Madras Presidency Telugus fought alongside the Telugus from Telangana against rural landlords who helped uphold the Nizam's rule. In one of his interviews, well-known communist activist Burgula Narsing Rao provided historical and present-day context to the term 'Andhra'.

Sometime in 1920–21, for the first time, an organization was established in Hyderabad by the name 'Jana Sangham'. The term 'Andhra' used here at that time represented symbolically an awareness of one's own language, for example Telugu. You see Telugu, Telangana and Andhra—these distinctions are so prominent today. They are at the forefront. But the use of the term Andhra at that time signified a 'Telugu' awareness of one's own language and culture.[17]

But early ruptures between the Telangana and Andhra Telugu-speakers foreshadowed the statehood movement that would define the state's politics for many decades in the future. Burgula Ramakrishna Rao, uncle of Burgula Narsing Rao and the second (and last) chief minister of Hyderabad state, spoke of the tensions that surfaced during the Razakar agitation.

He expressed his trepidation regarding the merger in a letter to then president of the Indian National Congress, U.N. Dhebar. He lamented:

> Although the language is common, there are instances that there is no love lost between the Telugus in both the states. The classical example of this mutual dislike can be found in the attitude of Andhra officers during the Razakar agitation and immediately after the accession of Hyderabad. While they say the Marathi, Kannada and other officers were comparatively kind to the people of Hyderabad, Andhra officers were particularly harsh and unrelenting. There are bad memories left. These memories are so fresh in the minds of the Telanganites that they do not want to be at the mercy of their brethren in Andhra.[18]

Within the Telugu-speaking contingents, differences were beginning to creep in about the future of the movement. According to Narsing Rao, the party leadership also got hijacked by Andhraites like Puchalapalli Sundarayya.[19] He believed that the Madras Presidency Telugus wanted to continue the armed struggle even if it meant more casualties among the Telangana cadres on the ground.[20]

By 1951, the Telangana Rebellion was called off. With many of Hyderabad's communists now a part of the democratic setup, leftist writers and party members were doing their bit to not only help the communists function as an opposition, but to also use their talents to further communal amity.

In the following year though, the son-of-the-soil versus outsider issue that has always reared its head in the Deccan since the pre-Asaf Jahi era, surfaced within Hyderabad state.

About 150 kilometres northeast of Hyderabad city, students in Warangal raised slogans like 'Idli sambar[21] ghar ko jao (Idli sambar go home)' and 'Non-Mulkis go back!' against non-Mulki outsiders.[22] These outsiders were mostly Telugu speakers from the Madras Presidency, who had monopolized jobs in academia and government jobs, thereby limiting the employment prospects for native 'Mulkis'.

This hostility, however, did not make Hyderabad city less of an attraction for the Andhraite Telugu population. They wanted the former Asaf Jahi seat of government as a capital for their own Telugu state, as the Tamil population of the Madras Presidency made it clear to the province's Telugu speakers that Madras was to be the capital of Tamil Nadu.[23] Plus, Potti Sriramulu's loud cries for a Telugu-speaking state began getting louder before his death. His demise resulted in the formation of an Andhra state carved out of the Madras Presidency in 1953. Merging the two Telugu-speaking territories increasingly looked like a reality. Journalist and author Venkateswara Rao Adiraju wrote in his book *Telangana: Saga of a Tragic Struggle* that Andhra leaders had also warned of the bogey of Muslim domination if a separate Telangana was to surface.[24]

But as talk of creating new Indian states on a linguistic basis gained more ground, Habib-ur-Rahman, Srinivas Lahoti, Raj Bahadur Gour and Abid Ali Khan left for New Delhi, where they met Jawaharlal Nehru.

They understood that the creation of Andhra Pradesh was paramount. Prime Minister Nehru and Education Minister Maulana

Abul Kalam Azad could help make it happen, but both would require some convincing.

Cleansing the Palate

Although not fond of its feudal establishment, Hyderabad's composite culture had a fan in the Indian Prime Minister.[25] The *Siasat* co-founder lobbied the PM for a trifurcation of Hyderabad upon linguistic basis. Marathi-speaking territories—today referred to as Marathwada—would become a part of Maharashtra, while Karnataka would get the state's Kannada-speaking population. The Telangana region would then be merged with the Madras Presidency's Telugu-speaking portions that had constituted a separate Andhra state in 1953.

'*Dono zang-alood khanjar se zakhmi hai* (Both Hindus and Muslims have fresh wounds from an old, rusty knife). An influx of a new Andhra population was needed to heal those fractures between Hindus and Muslims.'—that is what his father had told the Prime Minister, Zaheer Ali Khan shared.

The Prime Minister was convinced, but he left it to the delegation to get Maulana Azad, India's first education minister, on board. The delegates knew that being a diabetic, Maulana made frequent bathroom trips during long work days. Catching him while he returned to his office from the bathroom would be the best time to sell this idea.

When they made their pitch, all Azad had to say initially was, 'Why?'

Khan stressed the need for new blood in Hyderabad city and the Telugu areas of the state. The Deccan had been a fertile ground for the convergence of various linguistic and religious traditions; yet the Police Action and Partition had fostered deep-seated acrimony among both Hyderabad's Hindus and Muslims. Azad asked about the fate of Urdu and the Deccan's composite culture.

'Under the reign of Muslims, Hindi flourished to different extents all over the country,' Abid responded, 'Hindu culture did not wither away. We still have the right, ability and responsibility to keep Urdu alive.'

While Khan and the rest of his delegate members might have cast their lot for a Telugu state, other Telangana leaders like Burgula Ramakrishna Rao, K.V. Ranga Reddy, Chenna Reddy and J.V. Narsing Rao were not as enthusiastic.

To prevent discrimination in recruitment for government services and to ensure equal expenditures towards both the Telangana and Andhra regions, Ramakrishna Rao, Ranga Reddy, Chenna Reddy and Narsing Rao signed what was known as the Gentlemen's Agreement with Andhra leaders B. Gopal Reddy, N. Sanjeeva Reddy, G. Lachanna and Alluri Satyanarayana Raju.[26]

Despite this agreement, overrepresentation of Andhraites in the Public Works and Public Health departments, Panchayat Raj and various other domains continued to be rampant. Between 1958 and 1968, ten polytechnic colleges were established in the Andhra region whereas the Telangana region did not get more than the two it already had.[27]

This, and other blatant violations of the pact, reinforced the feeling among Telanganites that they needed their own state. But Abid Ali Khan did not share this sentiment.

The Gulf and Gazetted Officers

Zahid Ali Khan remembered his days as a student in the early 1960s. It was a time when he used to play pro-Telangana songs on the car's stereo. 'One day the slogan "*Jai Jai Telangana*! (Long live Telangana!)" blared out loud while my father sat beside me during a car ride,' Zahid told me, 'he ejected the tape and threw it out of the car.'

The sentiment on the streets was heating up. Burgula Ramakrishna Rao's words turned out to be prophetic. Money earmarked for irrigation projects did not end up benefiting Telangana. Non-Mulkis continued being preferred for government jobs. The Kothagudem Thermal Power Plant debacle was an example of this when 175 Telangana employees among 1,400 workers were retrenched. And with the Telangana Non-Gazetted Officers Association as well as OU students pushing for Mulki jobs, the first struggle for a separate state was well and truly underway.

The attention of *Siasat*'s founders was elsewhere, though. They had their own community to worry about. The paper steered clear of publishing anything other than news of the casualties.

Muslims, in general, stayed away from the 1969 agitation for statehood.[28] They were in the midst of readjusting to the reality of their minority status. They had not fully recovered from the 1948 tragedy that caused this realignment. The MIM, which had been revived as the All India Majlis Ittehad-ul-Muslimeen, also kept its distance from the separate Telangana campaign in 1969. In return for doing so, Kasu Brahmananda Reddy, then chief minister of Andhra Pradesh, promised to return the confiscated Dar-us-Salaam headquarters to the party.[29]

Police Action and the Telangana Rebellion had injected a sensitivity in poets, musicians, humourists and writers. *Siasat* patronized artist associations by publishing the work of their members and advertising events at which their talents were to be showcased. Artists' guilds like the Fine Arts Academy and its literary wing, Zinda Dillan-e-Hyderabad, held mushairas[30] where witty poets like Sarwar Danda gave Hyderabadis reasons to laugh after a lot of tears had been shed.[31]

Art did provide a balm to soothe the wounds, but it could not address the problem of sustenance. For that, there were organizations like the Society for Employment and Training in Twin Cities (SETWIN).[32]

Things slowly began to look up for Hyderabadi Muslims. The private sector in India was still nascent. But opportunities came from Gulf countries, whose oil-rich economies required all sorts of white-collar and blue-collar professionals. Advertisements for employment in the Gulf were plastered all over the jobs section in *Siasat*. Many of these advertisements mentioned that vocational training certificates issued by SETWIN would be accepted as a qualification.[33]

The diaspora was important to Abid Ali Khan. At overseas events where he was often invited to speak, he would mention how moved he was by ordinary Hyderabadis who migrated to foreign countries to make a living for their families. In the 1990s, he travelled to Saudi Arabia, Kuwait and England to commemorate Hyderabad's 400th year of existence as a city.

'In the Sunday edition of *Siasat*, he printed articles by those who had migrated to the United States, the United Kingdom, Holland and the Gulf,' Zaheer said. 'This would enable other younger people to learn about more lucrative and readily available paths to success abroad. These articles had information about how these youngsters should go about pursuing opportunities. They would also have first-hand information about what awaited them there,' added Zaheer.

Remittances from the Gulf enabled many families to admit their children into the city's premier institutions. However, the influx of Gulf money also brought back extravagant spending habits. It reminded Abid of the Muslim nobles' excesses in the run-up to the fall of Hyderabad. Zaheer disclosed, 'The ridiculous expenditure on ultra-lavish weddings and other celebrations that went on late into the night affected him on a deep level.'

This is why Abid Ali Khan and P.V. Pavitran, the Hyderabad city police commissioner, organized a conference on financial literacy for those who received and sent remittances.

Meanwhile, *Siasat* and the MIM, which at one time did not see eye-to-eye on Hyderabad's independence, had mended relations. The party itself had undergone a change in leadership and direction. Their activities were focused on advancing the cause of Muslims in the public sphere. *Siasat* provided coverage to the MIM and amplified its voice.

Becoming a Powerhouse

As Muslims in Hyderabad began rebuilding their lives, *Siasat* became a voice to be reckoned with. Today, the print circulation is 32,000.[34]

Its e-paper was launched by Prime Minister Manmohan Singh in 2004. An English edition, completely online, went live in 2011.

In its early days, Jigar had functioned both as the editor and delivery boy. Both Abid and him rode bicycles to work. Till his death in 1997, Jigar looked after the editorial duties, while Abid handled the business and marketing side of the publication.

Abid Ali Khan's grandson, Amer Ali Khan, who is currently *Siasat*'s editor-in-chief, is still in awe of how Jigar performed the work of six people. Up at the crack of dawn, he would first get to publishing letters to the editor. Being among the first Indian outlets to break the news about the joint British-French-Israeli invasion of Egypt in 1956 helped the newspaper establish journalistic credibility.[35]

When he joined the publication in 1954, Zahid Ali Khan worked more closely with his father on the administrative and business end.

Siasat continued to promote and support secular viewpoints. Zaheer Ali Khan told me about how Prime Minister P.V. Narasimha Rao took exception to when the paper published a certain remark by him that was seen as singling out Muslims. 'Even though the paper had reported him saying that molten lead should be poured into the ears of those who tuned their sets to Pakistan's radio channel, Rao paid his respects to Abba when he died,' he recalled.

From 1956 to 1982, the newspaper operated at a loss. But again, it was the diaspora that changed their fortunes. They were fanned out across the West and the Middle East. The ones who had prospered in North America and England had purchased properties and acquired American, Canadian or British citizenship. The NRIs who were based in the Middle East used to travel back more often to Hyderabad and spend freely in the city. Advertisers were keen on reaching these potential customers earning in riyals and dirhams. This certainly helped with increasing circulation from 10,000 in 1976 to 44,000 twenty years later.[36]

As the paper's fortunes began looking up, the Ram Janmabhoomi movement that lead to the Babri Masjid's demolition cast a pall of gloom among the Muslim population around the country. Now that it was a profitable institution, *Siasat* undertook relief efforts for those who had suffered during the riots.

Since the early 1990s, India's liberalization had provided fillip to the IT sector in the country. In 1995, Chandrababu Naidu of the Telugu Desam Party (TDP) dislodged his father-in-law, Nandamuri Tarakarama Rao (NTR), to become Andhra Pradesh's chief minister. Naidu ensured that Hyderabad became a major centre of this IT boom. *Siasat*'s founders knew that for Muslims to be a part of this, they would need to be proficient in English. To this day, many still venture to the *Siasat* office to improve their English so they can compete for jobs in the technology hub that is HITEC City.

Keeping the Promise Made to Maulana Azad

Within HITEC City also lies the proof of Abid Ali Khan honouring the pledge that he made to India's first education minister. Abid was a member of the Gujral Committee for the Promotion of Urdu. Based on this committee's recommendations, a conversation began around establishing an Urdu-medium university as early as 1972.[37]

Raj Bahadur Gour and Abid Ali Khan, classmates in OU lobbied hard for their city to be the home of this Urdu-medium institution. In the mid-1990s, when Chandrababu Naidu promised to allot land for what A.G. Noorani deems as the inheritor of OU's legacy, it would only be a few more years before Maulana Azad National Urdu University came to fruition.

But Abid Ali Khan would not live to see this as he passed away in 1992. His son Zahid then took over. Not too long after that P.V. Narasimha Rao offered the chance to start an Urdu newspaper with text published in the Devanagri script. By opting to not forgo the Urdu script, he declined Rao's proposition,[38] and thereby upheld the promise his father made to Maulana Azad.

'*Acche Din*' Come alongside a New State

In 2001, the dormant Telangana struggle received a boost when one of Chandrababu Naidu's closest companions broke away to form his own political party. The Telangana Rashtra Samithi party (TRS) came into existence with the promise of a new state, which Zaheer Ali Khan endorsed whole-heartedly. In 2009, his brother Zahid told him in jest, 'Abba's soul must be aching right now. He helped create Andhra Pradesh, and you support Telangana.'

Zaheer responded, 'Bhai, at that time, a united Telugu state served a purpose. The old wounds needed to be healed. The side effect of this was that Muslims were no longer viewed as hegemons. Andhra's political elite now lorded over them.'

On the cusp of Telangana's birth as the twenty-ninth state of India, Zahid Ali Khan was a part of the TDP. But the party's alignment with the Bharatiya Janata Party (BJP) in Andhra Pradesh prompted him to sever ties as a party member.

Full Circle

Zahid Ali Khan's allegiance to the TDP carried forward, in a sense, his father's commitment to the united Andhra Pradesh cause. Today, his son Amer Ali Khan is carrying forward his grandfather's legacy in a more literal sense—as chief editor of *Siasat*. In late August, I went to see Amer at the *Siasat* Urdu office, a stone's throw from Moazam Jahi Market.

I rarely ventured to this building even though the office of the online English edition, where I worked for over a year, is a mere twenty-minute drive away. Right across from the Ramakrishna theatre in Abids, I walked into the lane sandwiched between the Abid Ali Khan Centenary Hall on the left and the main office building on the right.

Amer's office was on the second floor, one story above his grandfather's old one. It exuded an old-world charm not found in the glossy cabins of corporate media houses. Reporters popped in and out of the room as we spoke, shooting story ideas and queries at Amer, who seemingly made spot decisions with a shake or nod of his head. With his portly frame, darting eyes and assured manner, Amer gave off the sense of a prosperous man who was at ease juggling the many balls he had up in the air. One of the more recent ones include fulfilling his duties as a member of the Telangana Legislative Council.

Another thing Amer seems to have inherited from his grandfather is his outspokenness and lack of fear of authority. At a conclave sponsored by Indian Muslims for Civil Rights in August 2022, Amer had thundered, 'Muslims do not need to show how loyal we are to this country to a *chowkidar*,'[39] referring to Prime Minister Narendra Modi's self-description as a watchman who would not permit corruption in the country.

In 2022, Amer got a call from the office of Anurag Thakur, the Union Minister of Information and Broadcasting, in the second Modi government (2019–2024). Not long before, Thakur had led chants of '*Goli maaro desh ke gaddaron ko* (Kill the traitors within this nation)' at a rally in Delhi, referring to the Muslim protestors who were protesting against the discriminatory nature of the *Citizenship Amendment Act*.[40]

'I asked the assistant, "*Wafadaar ku desh ke gaddaron se kya kaam?* (What work can a loyalist have to do with traitors?)"' Amer told me in his office. The swagger with which Amer relayed the line to me in Dakhani is untranslatable. But behind the swagger, Amer was disturbed by the way the winds were blowing in the country.

'When *Siasat* was formed, the objective was to signal people to not leave Hyderabad,' he specified.

'Now they are asking us to prove our citizenship. Parliamentary figures stated that 800,000 high-net-worth individuals are leaving India for foreign countries. These people are running, whereas the Muslims who had the chance to leave in 1947 are still here.'

In 2022, Amer, along with other editors from Urdu media, were invited by the I&B ministry for a meeting at Shastri Bhawan in New Delhi. 'They asked us to introduce ourselves, mention our publication and say a few words,' Amer mentioned. When his turn came, he only mentioned his name and *Siasat*. But an official insisted that he continue to say a few words.

Not one to couch his true feelings, Amer told me that he brought up the issues that editors from Delhi, Uttar Pradesh and Bihar were afraid to openly acknowledge—the low rate offered by the BJP for newspaper advertisements, and their distaste for the ruling dispensation's treatment of the Muslim community.

'I said, "I will not talk about advertisements because we have crossed Rs 2 million in Ramzan.[41] But your communal BJP will give ads at Rs 18 per centimetre of column space when the TRS was willing to pay Rs 250."' Amer then mentioned that he directly confronted Thakur for his incendiary statements. The tension in the room could have been cut with a knife. Thakur tried to defuse the situation by deflecting responsibility, saying that someone else had spewed the venom.

When I was writing up my notes after meeting Amer, I recalled an incident I read about in the anthology *Aap Ki Tareef*, authored by Mehboob Hussain Jigar's brother Mujtaba Hussain. In it, Mujtaba described Abid Ali Khan's dissatisfaction with the way meeting minutes were compiled by the Urdu Promotion Board. B. Shankaranand, who at that time was the education minister, presided over these deliberations.

At one meeting, Abid Ali Khan took a small, portable tape recorder and openly criticized Shankaranand, 'I take exception to the disorganized manner in which the education minister has these meeting minutes compiled,'[42] he pointed out.

Reportedly, the minister asked his officers to rewrite the action items in the form of promises that Abid Ali Khan could hold the education minister to. The officers were made to apologize for their shoddiness. Back in the office, Amer was not done with his anecdotes about Anurag Thakur. In July 2022, the BJP held its conclave in Hyderabad after eighteen years.

When Rani Chotrani, a reporter from *Siasat*, had a couple of minutes with Thakur after his press conference, he told her, 'Your editor is a thorough gentleman.' Chotrani got Thakur on the phone with Amer, who invited him home for biryani. Thakur let him know he could not make it on that trip.

Amer Ali Khan, grandson of Abid Ali Khan, then looked me in the eye and said with genuine warmth, 'The offer for Thakur Saab is open. Whenever he is in the city, we will be happy to serve him biryani.'

Umar Faruq Quadri: From Jagirdar to Jamaati

نشاں یہی ہے زمانے میں زندہ قوموں کا
کہ صبح و شام بدلتی ہیں اِن کی تقدیریں
— علامہ اقبال

Nishaan yahi hai zamaane mein zinda qaumon ka
Ki subh-o-shaam badalti hain inn ki taqdeerein

It is a major sign in our times of living nations and communities
That their fortunes can change overnight

—Allama Iqbal

FOR HYDERABADIS AND outsiders alike, the mention of the Falaknuma area in Old City evokes the name of the majestic palace that the Taj Hotels turned into a luxury hotel in 2010. This royal residence of the sixth Nizam Mahbub Ai Khan, first belonged to Paigah noble Viqar-ul-Umra.

Legend has it that when Mahbub Ali Pasha was invited by this high-ranking aristocrat, who served as the state's Prime Minister, to his abode, he was so enamoured by the palace that he stayed there for a month. Viqar-ul-Umra got the hint. He then offered the sixth Nizam his home, for which Mahbub Ali Pasha paid him Rs 2 million.[1]

But it is not the rich history of the luxury heritage hotel or its erstwhile noble resident—whose predecessor and fellow Paigah noble Asma Jah traces his lineage back to the Sufi saint Baba Farid Ganjshakar[2]—that brought me to this part of the Old City.

A ten-minute drive away from Falaknuma Palace is the house of Halima Bi, who has a Police Action story. Her family had to leave behind their feudal estate in Latur district, which is in present-day Maharashtra but was once a part of the Nizam's dominions.

Along with Latur, which was home to Qasim Razvi, the then Majlis-Ittehad-ul-Muslimeen chief and Razakar commander, other Marathi- and Kannada-speaking districts had borne the brunt of Police Action-related violence.

I first came to know of Halima Bi through her grand-nephew, Umar Faruq Quadri, who was the Students' Union President at the Maulana Azad National Urdu University (MANUU) in 2019.

Umar and I were introduced to each other by a mutual friend at MANUU. In a campus filled with students from Bihar, Uttar Pradesh and Jammu and Kashmir, his local accent stood out. Within the first few minutes of that introduction, he told me about the vast tracts of land his grandparents used to own in their native Latur district. Overnight, Police Action had pushed his family into a life of hardship in Mominabad, which ended up becoming a part of Maharashtra, and then Ichoda in present-day Telangana.

Quadri's story was fascinating to me, because it did not feature the Gulf the way it did in the stories of many Hyderabadi Muslim families that had been touched by Police Action. Instead, the religious organization known as the Jamaat-e-Islami (JI) played a central role in the arc of the Quadris' lives.

A Little Marathwada/Hyderabad–Karnataka in Old City

Umar had arranged for me to sit down with Halima Bi at his paternal uncle's house to chat about the old days. For someone like me who has mostly spent time in the 'New City' whenever in Hyderabad, the Falaknuma area in the southern part of purana sheher (Old City) is a different world. When wandering around in the Old City, researching features about Urdu bookstores or just visiting my mother's extended family, I usually only venture through the northern parts of purana sheher.

While parking my car after both of us arrive at his uncle's home, I told Umar that this area within purana sheher seemed a lot more spacious than the parts I was more familiar with. He agreed that the landscape in this area was different—the neighbourhoods close to the Charminar had flatter terrain, but Falaknuma is rather hilly.

A group of children were playing football outside the house of Umar's paternal uncle. When one of them kicked the ball so high that it ended up on the roof of a house, another child yelled, '*Ball kaado wahan se!*'

I asked Umar what the boy meant by 'kaado'. He responded, 'It means "nikalo" (take it out).' It was not a word that was ordinarily used by the Dakhani-speakers from Hyderabad city, but it was commonly used by people from the Marathi- and Kannada-speaking districts of the Nizam's dominion—places like Aurangabad, Osmanabad and Gulbarga. The Falaknuma area is home to many families from the Marathi- and Kannada-speaking districts of the erstwhile princely state.

Speaking to Quadri's family, I realized that the difference between my Urdu-centric Dakhani and the more Marathi-influenced one spoken by them was starker than I imagined. People from Hyderabad city can be snobbish about their tongue, being quick to dismiss the dialects from the Deccan region as rough and unsophisticated. But there are many pleasures to be had in these dialects flecked with Telugu, Marathi and Kannada—as often evidenced in mazahiya mushairas (humour poetry gatherings), where even the most urban poets have no qualms about peppering their verses with Marathi-sounding words like 'minje' instead of the Hindi-Urdu 'ma'ane' (meaning).

'Humaare Ghar Mein "Angrezaan" Ghuss Gaye The'

'*Humaare ghar mein Angrezaan ghuss gaye the. Razakaaron ku gher re the aur jeepaan mein daal ko leko jaa re the* (Englishmen stormed into our house. They were rounding up Razakars and shoving them into jeeps),' narrated Halima Bi. Her slender frame and moderately frail voice complemented the stoic tone.

Like Punjabi, the Dakhani dialects of Urdu add the 'aan' to turn any singular noun into a plural one. The '*daal ko*' instead of '*daal ke* (put in, insert)' intrigued me as that sounded closer to a more old-fashioned style of speaking Dakhani. I was baffled by Halima Bi's use of the word 'Angrezaan', which, if taken literally, would mean the English. But Umar clarified that she was not referring to English troops, who were long gone by the time the Indian military had started rounding up the Razakars. As an old-school denizen of Hyderabad, she referred to anyone who was not native to the princely state as the foreigner, the 'Angrez'.

This pride in her origins was also reflected in her use of the word 'watan', which ordinarily refers to the nation in Urdu. But Halima Bi used it to refer to Bamini, her hometown in Latur district, which was then a part of the Marathi-speaking parts of Hyderabad state.

Umar's paternal grandparents were from a landed family that had 50 acres of land in the Bamini village of Latur. There, the family lived on a large estate where animals roamed free.

They were also the descendants of a Sufi saint, which bestowed another layer of prestige on the family. Halima Bi mentioned that her father, Umar Shah Quadri, had been a disciple of Hussain Shah Baba whose shrine is located 10 kilometres northeast of Pune.

In 1948, their lives were overturned one afternoon. As part of Operation Polo, the Indian Army was chasing down Razakars. Latur district was a stronghold of the group, given that Qasim Razvi was from the same area.

Without much emotion, Halima Bi narrated how the army entered their house, grabbed members of her family and marched them all up to the Haqqani Baba Dargah, a Sufi shrine on top of a hill near their home. She was certain they were all going to be killed. But some of her family members got on their knees and begged to be spared. Miraculously, they were set free. They made their way back to the house. In the fracas, Umar Shah Quadri's leg got fractured. That fateful afternoon, he picked up a limp that would stay with him for the rest of his days.

After the incident, Umar Shah Quadri decided to take his family to Mominabad, about 200 kilometres northeast of Aurangabad. I asked Halima Bi if her family was able to take any belongings with them. Diluting her impassiveness with a bit of humour, she retorted, '*Maathi kuch bhi nahin leke jaa sake apan* (We could not take diddly squat with us).'

For three years, they lay low in a Muslim-dominated locality. 'The Hindus helped us out a lot with food and shelter. The nomadic lambadas[3] who lived in the bushes also made sure no harm came to us.' Halima Bi remembered.

Despite the helping hands, they knew that they would be safer in the northern Telangana districts of Hyderabad state.

The Jamaat's Hyderabad Connection

Beyond the basic differences between sectarian groups like Sunnis and Shiites, or even sub-sectarian ones between Ismailis and Bohras, I do not have much of a grasp on the finer distinctions between the various branches of Islam. More so, I am not acquainted with the Deobandi school of thought that influenced Maulana Maududi, the founder of Jamaat-e-Islami. Interestingly enough, the JI founder was also a Syed from the Sufi silsila (order) like Umar's grandfather.

The last name Quadri denotes a family pedigree that goes back to a mystic order of priests that is distinct from the three other major Sufi orders: Chishtiya, Suhrawardiya and Naqshbandi. The common factor among them is that they all trace their lineage back to Prophet Muhammad.

Syed Abul Ala Maududi, the founder of the JI, was born in Aurangabad. From a young age, Maududi immersed himself in the study of political and religious texts. His writings, published in his monthly journal *Tarjuman-al-Quran*, got him noticed by the poet and philosopher Muhammad Iqbal.[4]

Iqbal was impressed with the clarity and sagacity that this promising Hyderabadi writer and thinker displayed. Hence, he invited Maududi to Lahore. Finding him had narrowed his search for a competent individual to spearhead an Islamic centre of learning called Dar-ul-Islam. Chaudhry Niaz Ali Khan, one of the poet's protégés, allocated land and funds for Dar-ul-Islam in Pathankot, in present-day Punjab.[5] In 1941, three years after Iqbal's death, the Jamaat-e-Islami came into existence as an organization. Five years later, Maududi spoke against the Muslim League by saying that the fate of Pakistan would 'lay in the hands of those who believed in a secular mode of politics and state'.[6] In 1947, when Pathankot became a part of independent India, Maududi migrated to Lahore.

As the 1947 Indo–Pak war over Kashmir raged on and both countries reeled under the aftermath of the Partition violence, the question of Hyderabad's future was close to Maududi's heart.

According to a letter he sent to Qasim Razvi in December 1947, Maududi knew about the calamities that awaited the people of his native land if the ruling and feudal classes did not take stock of certain realities. He felt that it would only be a matter of time before Indian democracy supplanted the monarchy. And that is why he wrote a letter to Razvi imploring him to negotiate with the Indian government for terms of accession before things got worse with New Delhi.[7]

Mohammed Yunus, Syed Abdul Qader and Mohammed Khurshid, who formed a small contingency of the Jamaat in Hyderabad, took this letter to the MIM's headquarters in the Dar-us-Salaam area of Hyderabad city. The Majlis chief did not even offer the courtesy of meeting them, despite the fact that they had secured an appointment with Razvi.[8] But one of Maududi's prophecies would come true soon.

'The state's forces, police, courts and administration will not be able to hold their own in the event of a conflict with the Indian Union,'[9] he had written.

He had also correctly warned, 'The rich and powerful have always watched out for their own ilk and interests. To avoid the same fate as the Nawab of Junagadh, they will cut deals with the new establishment to save themselves.'[10]

Had Qasim Razvi heeded the advice of Maududi, life would have perhaps been different for Umar Shah Quadri. Even though Maududi's words did not find takers among various aristocrats and princes, his teachings would play a major role in the lives of Quadri's descendants.

One among Many Schools of Islamic Thought

Being a member of the Jamaat's student wing known as the Students Islamic Organisation (SIO), Umar answered some of my questions about the organization in which his father was an initiated member.

As per the Deobandi and certain other schools of Islamic thought, certain Sufi practices such as paying obeisance to saints,[11] visiting their shrines,[12] and certain forms of devotional acts such as qawwali music[13] are deemed as human innovations that are not prescribed by the Quran and Sunna (traditions and practices of the Prophet Muhammad that are exemplars for Muslims to follow).

For many, sometimes merely stepping into a dargah, paying respects to a saint, and even listening to the soulful music that qawwals perform at these spiritual sites—all amount to deviations from the true path of Islam.

Though Umar does listen to qawwalis merely as a way to pass time, it is clear that he has come to eschew shrine culture.

During our third meeting, Umar gently nudged me to read Maududi's book *Khilafat-o-Mulukiyat* (Caliphate and Kingdom) in Urdu.

In a Muslim-majority country like Pakistan, the JI's objectives are to bring governance and society on par with Islamic law. On the other hand, Quadri told me how the Jamaat-e-Islami-e-Hind is an apolitical body that came into existence in 1948 under the leadership of Maulana Abul Lais Nadwi. Only in 1952 at the all-India level congregation in Hyderabad would the smaller contingents of the Jamaat merge with JI Hind. However, it would be some time before the group's Deccan chapter carried out their da'wa (the practice of policy of conveying the message of Islam to non-Muslims).

At first, the People's Democratic Front, through which many communists contested the first Hyderabad state assembly elections, did its part in restoring the morale of Muslims in whom they had a voter base early on.[14] But the re-emergence of the Majlis Ittehad-ul-Muslimeen as the All-India Majlis Ittehad-ul Muslimeen in the late 1950s would change that.[15] However, unlike the JI, the MIM did not enter the rural districts of the Telangana region due to the party being banned after Police Action. The JI as well as other organizations like Tamir-e-Millat had already began relief and rehabilitation work in the wake of Operation Polo.

Not too long after the meeting where Umar asked me to read *Khilafat-o-Mulukiyat*, I happened to be at the Alamgiri Mosque, which is close to my maternal grandparents' former home in Masab Tank. I asked the Imam there about what he thought of Maududi's seminal text.

He advised, '*Padho kitaab. Leken apne khayaalaat mat badlo* (Do give it a read but do not change your thoughts based on that).'

Leaving Mominabad for Ichoda

A few days after my conversation with Halima Bi, Umar and I met in the JI's office off Chatta Bazaar Road in the Old City. I got there after walking through a bylane off Jamal Market Road, which was dotted with invitation card designing and printing centres.

The overall Chatta Bazaar–Jamaal Market area is more familiar territory to me compared to Falaknuma. One of my go-to shops for Urdu literature, Huda Books, is close by.

I asked Umar about how his great-grandfather had survived in a new city with the rest of his family. Turns out, it was his Sufi lineage that came in handy. 'My great-grandfather was of the Barelvi background of the Quadriya order. He literally became a Sufi faqeer.'[16]

The spread of Islam in the subcontinent saw the intermingling of many different traditions, one of them being caste. Muslims of the subcontinent adopted many characteristics of Hindu hierarchies, which resulted in a similar stratification among them as well.

Being a Syed, Umar's clan has a high standing in the topmost priestly group in the so-called Ashraf layer. As a wandering, homeless saint who had a limp, people gave Umar Shah Quadri money when he asked for it. This continued in Ichoda as well.

As was a common practice then, Halima Bi then got married to an Ichoda native who was also a Syed. When he told me the name of his paternal grandfather, a part of me anticipated that Quadri would mention his Najeeb-al-Tarfain (which literally translates to 'noble on both sides') status that many north Indian and Pakistani 'Double Syeds' sometimes proudly parade. While not to the extent of north India, caste does rear its head among urban Hyderabadis as well. But other than to lend context to his family's origins, Umar did not even mention his 'Syed-ness'—at least not till I asked about it later.

The union between Halima Bi and her husband took place around the 1956 merger of Hyderabad state's Telangana region with the former Telugu-speaking Rayalaseema and coastal districts of the Madras Presidency.

Sustenance and, more importantly, education were among the concerns for them at the time. Luckily, the family benefitted from the generosity of a Reddy[17] landlord in Ichoda. As a mark of respect for Umar Shah Quadri, the landlord granted them a small parcel of land. Quadri used the land to build a chilla—a retreat where saints performed the practice of penance and solitude—in honour of Sufi saint Hazrat Mahboob Subhani, also known as Ghouse-e-Paak.

Education: A Stepping Stone at This Stage

On this piece of land, they had a small space that ensured their basic shelter was taken care of. Educated in a Telugu-medium school up to the fourth grade, Halima Bi's brother Mohammed Shah Quadri ended up getting a job in the postal department at a salary of Rs 100 per month. Her younger brother Ismail also joined the same department.

But the Quadris still yearned for a sense of community and belonging. Umar asserted, 'The stigma of my great-grandfather being a beggar haunted my family. While not to the degree that they did before, some people back home still see me and my immediate kin in the same light that they saw my grandfather. What other choice did he have to feed his family after the tragedy that befell him during Police Action?'

One would think priestly standing would perhaps endow them with social capital, but that was not the case. Instead, it kept people at arm's length. 'Another reason people did not want to associate with my family was that they still thought of them as faqeers, not in the spiritual sense but solely in the socioeconomic sense. When we started veering towards education, things slowly began to change a bit,' said Umar.

Enter the Jamaat

Umar's father, Sheikh Ahmed Quadri was born in the Telangana region in 1974. In the decades prior, the Jamaat had gradually expanded its presence in unified Andhra Pradesh. In 1977, it ramped up its activities after the Emergency imposed by then Prime Minister Indira Gandhi was lifted.

At educational centres, children were served breakfast before they were made to do one hour of math, Urdu and Quranic Arabic. Adults were given lessons in the Quran and religious scripture, with the Jamaat preferring an interpretation that it believed is devoid of innovation.

Two years after Umar's father completed his engineering diploma from a government college in the Boath Mandal of Adilabad district, he got married. In 1996, Umar was born. Ahmed Quadri performed menial jobs such as working as an electrician to make ends meet then.

Upon becoming active with the group, Umar's father learned Urdu and became fond of it. Learning it was imperative to consume and comprehend the Jamaat's literature. A little before Umar entered middle school, Sheikh Ahmed's family would enter the JI fold as they soon began attending the Jamaat's public programmes in Ichoda.

Umar remembered, 'When I was in the eighth grade, my father was taught to master the reading of Quranic Arabic. He did so with such zeal because he realized that he was so backward in terms of his own education. He felt that he was not "civilized". In order to better himself, he knew that he needed to learn those languages.'

It was around this time that the family began wiping out traces of their Sufi legacy. As ties with the Jamaat got stronger, Sufi practices would have no place in the Quadri household. Mohammed Shah Quadri fulfilled his father's wish to be buried next to his spiritual mentor, Ghouse-e-Paak. This was the family's final farewell to the Sufi identity that they had possessed for centuries.

With the formation of the Jamaat student wing, SIO, in 1982, Sheikh Ahmed's son would later be exposed to a world that he became a part of as an adult.

Junior Associates and SIO Stints, No Guarantors of Membership

Every Sunday, the SIO put together children's circle sessions through their Junior Associates programme for those between the ages five and fourteen. By teaching Islamic principles, storytelling and character development, it served a purpose to build a culture of engaging children in a religious environment.

Every Sunday, children also took part in a competition to see who was the best at singing hamds (devotional songs in praise of God). Umar did not have the best singing voice but he lacked stage fright. The Jamaat noticed his knack for expressing himself in both Telugu and Urdu. Attending state-level oratorial workshops would help him master both languages.

At the age of fourteen, as a ninth-grade student, he became the SIO unit secretary and he held onto that position till his second year of intermediate studies.

By this time, Sheikh Ahmed had become an active participant in Jamaat activities while also doing da'wa. Being an excellent Marathi speaker enabled him to carry out da'wa activities in Maharashtra. Through this preaching in regional languages, the organization was acting upon Maududi's advice from a historic speech he had given in Madras about eight decades ago. The JI founder knew that both the Jamaat and Muslims overall would be shooting themselves in the foot if it only relied on Urdu to spread its word.[18]

It was a long process to become a card-carrying member of the Jamaat. Extensive examination and moulding awaited a prospective member looking to join the parent organization. Umar told me that one had to wait a year before becoming a part of Jamaat's student wing.

While early engagement with youth wings like the SIO and Youth Islamic Circle might get an extra foot in the door with the committee that decides upon membership, it does not guarantee automatic entry into JI.

Within that long window, prospective members are ones who have worked towards a complete understanding of Islam according to the Quran and the Hadith (the corpus of the sayings and teachings of the Prophet), a proper Islamic character, a goal-oriented mindset, firm faith in God and his messenger and the ability to further the cause at a community level.[19]

Upon initiation into the main parent organization, a new member is made to recite the kalima, which affirms the oneness of God and Mohammed as his messenger, as a renewal of one's faith.[20] It took Sheikh Ahmed Quadri fifteen years to complete all these steps and become a full-fledged member of the Jamaat.

The long wait was worth it because the Quadris finally found in the Jamaat the thing that had eluded them since 1948—acceptance. The Jamaat, in a way, took the family under its wing—it would provide the assistance that would allow Umar and his sister to earn college degrees.

The JI as Benefactors

'People discriminated against us because of that "faqeer" label we got due to my great-grandfather who begged. But that did not matter to the JI,' Umar told me.

Umar wanted to serve society by joining the Indian Administrative Services, but that path seemed unlikely given the Quadris' economic predicament at that juncture. Better exposure and education avenues lay in Hyderabad city.

Around the time he was to go to college, the family had yet another setback. The state government's Department of Roads and Buildings accused the Quadri family of encroaching upon public property. The property that was gifted to them by the Reddy landlord was seized by the state. Sheikh Ahmed Quadri did not have the time and money to take the matter to the courts. He told his children to forget this issue and instead focus on their studies.

Just about a year after Telangana's formation and the victory of the BJP in the 2014 Lok Sabha Polls, Umar got admitted to the Babu Jagjivan Ram Degree College in the Narayanguda area of Hyderabad.

He explained, 'I knew that if I stayed away from home, my monthly expenditure would be between Rs 10,000 and Rs 15,000.'

The Jamaat student wing's state president came through for him and guaranteed him free SIO accommodation in the city.

'That help from Jamaat is why I was able to complete my graduation. The accommodation provided me with an environment where fellow SIO seniors were also pursuing higher education in the city,' Umar specified.

Hyderabad is where he gained more exposure. The SIO wanted him to become the face of the SIO at MANUU.

Exciting Times at Maulana's Namesake University

Other than the suicide of English and Foreign Languages University student Mudassir Kamran and the hanging of Afzal Guru, who was allegedly involved in the 2001 terrorist attack on the Indian Parliament, MANUU's student activism had been limited to internal issues like the lack of a dining mess. However, in 2016, the suicide of Rohith Vemula at the University of Hyderabad (also known as Hyderabad Central University) changed that. With the issue reverberating across the country, SIO members at MANUU had been energized by interacting with their counterparts.

When Umar arrived on campus, the SIO at MANUU was very active. Umar had been groomed to become the face of the group on campus. He hit the ground running when he helped found the Azad United Students' Federation (AUSF). Coming from an SIO background, where regionalism was non-existent, he noticed that divisions among students from Uttar Pradesh, Bihar and Jammu and Kashmir based on ethnicity or language were prevalent. A new students' organization with no political affiliation seemed like the need of the hour.

In early 2019, Umar led a successful campaign to become the president of the MANUU Students' Union. By the end of the year, protests against the Citizenship Amendment Act (CAA) were taking place all around the country.

Introduced in 2019, the CAA provided an automatic pathway to Indian citizenship for persecuted minorities from Afghanistan, Pakistan and Bangladesh. However, only Hindus, Sikhs, Buddhists, Jains, Zoroastrians and Christians were eligible for this—not Muslims. At the same time, the government was pushing for a National Register of Citizens (NRC). When implemented in Assam, the NRC had 1971 as a cut-off date. Those born before then would have to prove their bona fides via a birth certificate or any other official documents. The inability to gather any proof could have one declared as an illegal immigrant and sent to a detention camp.

The fact that not all Indians born before and after Independence were issued birth certificates—as is the practice today—instilled fear in many Muslims that they would be rendered stateless.[21] Non-Muslims who could not produce documentation would be eligible for regaining citizenship via the CAA but that legislation did not grant the same option to Muslims.

Universities all over the country rose in opposition to the CAA–NRC. MANUU, too, was a major site for these protests. Yet, even as Quadri and the MANUU-Students' Union vehemently protested against the authorities' brutal crackdown against the students at Jamia Milia Islamia and Aligarh Muslim University, the university's then chancellor sang a different tune.[22] Firoz Ahmed Bakht wrote an open letter to MANUU students using the university letterhead. The letter implored all Muslims to not fall into the clutches of the vested interests that were painting the CAA–NRC in a bad light.

'Kindly avoid coming onto the roads and strengthen the hands of your Prime Minister Modi, whom I can vouch for, is your well-wisher,' wrote Bakht. On a phone call in which Umar demanded an explanation from Bakht, he did not mince words when the chancellor asked them to concentrate on studies and steer clear of politics.

'But what else can we do when our country and its Constitution are in danger? That too when people like yourselves are selling India through your sycophancy,'[23] responded the then MANUU-SU president.

Be it holding a mirror to this highly placed university official, hosting the two Jamia Milia Islamia girls who shielded fellow students from the Delhi Police's lathi charge or shutting the university down in opposition to the Delhi riots, Umar and the other students exercised their constitutional right to peacefully protest.

Settled Down

Before graduating from MANUU in 2020, Umar's lively activism begged one question on my behalf. Did he want to get into politics?

Although he did express interest in serving society back then, he opted for a more lucrative path as an Urdu and English content moderator for Accenture in Hyderabad. The road to a stable income and career has nevertheless taught him a lot about his roots and how much of his past figures into his life today.

'I gained a sense of camaraderie and acceptance in the SIO and Azad United Students' Federation. A member's socioeconomic background or past did not matter to these two organizations. Knowing what I know now about my family's status before 1948 and where we are right now, I am more aware of the inequitable and un-Islamic ways of the feudal class my kin once belonged to,' reflected Umar.

The trajectory of the Quadri family shows how many layers there are to the Muslim experience after Police Action. While some went to the Gulf and others like Abid Ali Khan chose to work on communal harmony in Hyderabad, there were families like Umar's that had to discard certain facets of their pre-1948 identity. This renunciation went beyond simply shedding feudal hangovers of the past. One of the reasons they gravitated towards organizations like the Jamaat is the material and spiritual succour it offered in the aftermath of a traumatic experience.

West to East and Back

رہے گا راوی و نیل و فرات میں کب تک

تیرا سفینہ کہ ہے بحر بے کراں کے لئے

—علامہ اقبال

Rahega Ravi-o-Neel-o-Furat mein kab tak
Tera safeena ki hai beher-e-bekaraan ke liya

How long will your ship remain the in Ravi,
Nile and Euphrates? Your boat which is meant
to sail the ocean knows no bounds

—Allama Iqbal

Dar-us-Salaam, Razakar Central

My dear Razakars. Today is your biggest test as the blood
of Karbala's martyrs will adorn the horizons of the Deccan.
You will be subjected to seeing your Ali Akbars slaughtered
in front of your eyes. Hide your Ali Asghars in your arms.
It is time for your Abids to get orphaned, your Sheherbanos

39

widowed and your Qasims turned into grooms adorned with blood. We will have to do this to save ourselves from the slavery of India and thereby die a death that brings freedom.

The commandments of God stand high above the commandments of social law. I am very much aware of the arsenal that you are going to war with, and I also know which weapons the enemy has at its disposal. But remember that God's blessings are with you. With the arms in your hands, pave the road to eternal life.[1]

In his book, *Zawaal-e-Hyderabad*, former Razakar Mohammed Mazharuddin recalls these words of Qasim Razvi on 13 September 1948. As the Indian military entered the Nizam's dominions, the chief of the Majlis likened the conflict he was speaking of to the Battle of Karbala during which the Ummayad Caliphate martyred Imam Hussain.

Today, the elongated Dar-us-Salaam Road, on which the All-India Majlis Ittehad-ul-Muslimeen's (MIM) headquarters stands, is full of shops with glass windows, Sufi shrines, apartment buildings and Irani hotels. It still perplexes me to know that in 1948, the Razakar chief Qasim Razvi had goaded so many youths into laying down their lives against the more powerful Indian Army right across the very house my father grew up in.

My grandfather Mohammed Abdul Ghaffar, his wife, my late uncle and the rest of his extended family lived in a big house that once stood where the Krishna Residency apartment complex stands today. The saffron flags in the balconies and windows of Krishna Residency stand in contrast to the decrepit green wooden doors between the columns of Dar-us-Salaam's entrance.

Mohammed Abdul Ghaffar's life, too, would be altered by Razvi's rhetoric. At the time of Police Action, my grandfather was a captain in the Hyderabad Army's medical department.

Aurangabad: One of Qasim Razvi's Many Karbalas

Razvi had been obstinate about his stance of not negotiating with the Indian government. However, there were many like Maulana Maududi and the third last Prime Minister of Hyderabad, the Nawab of Chattari, who knew that his ambition of planting the Asaf Jahi flag on Delhi's Red Fort would not bode well for the princely state's people.

The Indian government, led by Jawaharlal Nehru, had been viewing Razvi's anti-accession rhetoric and Hyderabad Army Chief General Edroos's attempts to have arms smuggled into Hyderabad with increasing concern. But the murder of pro-Congress Urdu journalist Shoaibullah Khan was the tipping point. Nehru, who had been pushing for a peaceful solution to the stalemate, gave the order for the troops to march into Hyderabad.

It was not long before the Indian Army attacked the Aurangabad medical camp where my grandfather worked as a doctor. The army men lined up the personnel who worked there to shoot them in cold blood. Incredibly, the bullets missed my grandfather. But instead of giving away that the gunman had missed his mark, my grandfather pretended to be a lifeless corpse. The army men gathered the bodies on the floor, and like dirty laundry thrown into a washing machine, they tossed them into the back of a truck. The bodies were dumped in a deserted wasteland. When he felt the coast was clear, Ghaffar crawled out of the heap of bodies.

With stories of rapes, looting and massacres reaching Hyderabad city, my grandmother Aliya Begum, who was then pregnant with my father, presumed that her husband would never return. But one fine day, someone knocked on the door of her Dar-us-Salaam residence. The household help answered the door to see his employer standing in front of him. Even more astonished to see the presumed-dead man walking was Aliya Begum. About two months later, their second son, Majid, was born.

A year after his old employer, the Hyderabad State Forces, was disbanded, Ghaffar's daughter was born in 1949. Like many Muslims whose bread and butter came mostly from either the government or a feudal order that became yesterday's news overnight,[2] he was unsure of what the future held. Pakistan was an option, and not just for statesmen and journalists who had run afoul of the Indian government. Qualified, apolitical professionals who did not know what lay in store for them under a new regime were also choosing to migrate. Military, administrative, educational, medical and entrepreneurial jobs came in abundance with the formation of a new country and were for the taking.[3] In the year since India's independence, a link had developed between princely Hyderabad and Pakistan. Ghulam Muhammad, for instance, who had served as financial advisor to the Nizam, had been summoned by Jinnah to be a key member of the new country's finance ministry.

Hijrat or Homestay?

Crawling out from a heap of dead bodies is sure to take a toll on someone's psyche. Starting over in a new country would provide Ghaffar with a much-needed change of scenery. His elder brother and brothers-in-law were also contemplating futures there as well.

Ghaffar went as far as making a recce trip to Karachi. While there, he even selected some property to purchase in Pir Ilahi Baksh Colony, which had grown to be a hub of migrants from Hyderabad. Now, all that remained was to pack up his life in Hyderabad and make the move.

He returned home to learn that the plan had been scuttled. The thought of leaving their hometown and starting over had proved daunting for a lot of his in-laws. It was unthinkable to leave without his wife's sisters and their husbands. Additionally, the men had thought up alternate plans. Two of them were already on track to join the Civil Services. Another had decided to pursue a master's in the US.

Around this time, Ghaffar had his first heart attack.

With the Pakistan plan axed, he opened a clinic in the Hussaini Alam area. Gradually, he built a good reputation among residents of Dar-us-Salaam. My father told me about one of Ghaffar's patients, a Marwari lady whom he treated for severe burns. Moments before she passed, she asked for her doctor, hoping that his touch, which of course possessed no healing power, could save her.

Though not of a feudal background, Ghaffar had a bustling practice, three cars and a family of live-in servants. Life seemed to be getting back on track, especially after Aliya Begum gave birth to a pair of fraternal twins.

Things were looking up before tragedy struck.

1956: A Year of Separations

Ghaffar died of a cardiac arrest on 18 February 1956.

Ghaffar's elder brother Sattar and his brothers-in-law who were absorbed from the Hyderabad Civil Service into the Indian Administrative Service helped out their nephews with scholarships for elementary school. As for those two uncles who earlier lived with them—one moved in with his in-laws in their old neighbourhood of Begum Bazar; while the other found an independent home.

The five rooms now vacant in the massive Dar-us-Salaam house were given on rent at Rs 36 per month to students from Andhra, who were there to pursue postgraduate degrees.

Majid had been a student at Diamond Jubilee School, run by Ismaili Muslims, in Ghosha Mahal nearby. Soon, an uncle had him shifted to another English-medium school, Madrassa-e-Aliya. However, there were still money troubles in the family. My grandmother urged them to focus on academics, a task made doubly difficult by the fact that other relatives were hosting ghazal parties and many cousins were only paying lip service to studies.

My father told me of a time when his elder brother, Basit, secured admission to Osmania University to study medicine. The tuition for that year was Rs 300. 'We went to a Marwari in the Gulzar Hauz area near the Charminar to mortgage some jewellery to get money for his fees,' he recounted. The shopkeeper, recognizing them, asked where Aliya Begum had come from, to which she responded, 'Dar-us-Salaam'.

'When she told him "I am Ghaffar's widow", he gave her the money without holding any of her jewellery. He even told one of his helpers to escort us back home.'

A family friend named Ram Kishen owned a factory in their old neighbourhood of Begum Bazaar. My grandmother gathered some girls from the Dar-us-Salaam area to make sweets and pack them for sale at the factory. This brought in an extra Rs 50, which helped pay for her children's education.

Of Saintly Interventions and More Separations

The year 1969 saw Telangana's population rise up against Andhra domination. The disappointment of only 15 per cent of Telanganites being employed in the Kothagudem project and the allocation of funds towards irrigation schemes that would only benefit Andhra had set in. As a result, many clamoured for a separate state. Strikes brought a lot of educational institutions to a halt for about a year as students voiced their frustrations on the streets.

The tumult of this first agitation, along with other personal circumstances, would lead to one of Majid's uncles forgoing a promising public sector career. Ultimately, he would migrate to Pakistan. A few years after Police Action, he received a government scholarship to pursue a master's degree in structural engineering in America. When he returned, he took a well-paying job outside of Hyderabad in another state.

His plum post in the government caught the eye of a feudal family. They were considering him as a marriage prospect for their daughter. Even with land reforms being implemented in the 1950s, the fading aristocracy still held an appeal among many Hyderabadi families.

A chauffeur, servants and plush apartment were among the many perks of the government job. But it was still a step down from the aristocratic opulence his wife had grown up around. Furthermore, this new bride would be afflicted with homesickness, which contributed to the couple's decision to return home to Hyderabad.

By the time they moved back with their two kids, the initial Telangana struggle had turned the city into a mini war zone. Bandhs[4] were all too frequent. This tumultuous period, however, did not prevent her husband from putting his structural engineering education to use and starting his own construction business. But the Andhra real estate lobby, which was acquiring tracts of land all over the Hyderabad and Ranga Reddy districts, had grown more powerful. This nexus between AP's Coastal Andhra as well as Rayalaseema political factions and construction enterprises[5] reigned supreme within the city's real estate backdrop after 1969.

As a result, my father's uncle and his family left for Pakistan.

'My final year exams at Nizam College, where I got my first undergraduate degree, were postponed and my brother could not complete medical school on time because of the first Telangana agitation,' Majid stated.

Aliya Begum's money troubles continued through this period. By this time, the tenants who were students from Andhra had finished their degrees and left the house in Dar-us-Salaam. Four Sindhi brothers, who had crossed over to India from Karachi due to Partition, moved in soon after. The family owned radio stores and distributed chit funds. After being prompt with rent for a few months, they simply refused to pay.

'*Chhi! Aagayi kiraaya lene. Aap sab ko kya maalum? Humare paas kya nahin tha Karachi mein? Iss se badi kothi mein rehte the hum* (Eww! Here you are again for rent. You have no idea about what we used to have in Karachi! We lived in a bigger house than this),' Majid repeated the words his mother had to tolerate from her tenants.

Aliya Begum had to ensure that her sons did not get involved in disputes with the tenants, and instead could focus on their studies. When Ghaffar's brother, Sattar, spoke of selling the property, this ordeal served as an impediment. Even after emptying the house, the occupiers put a padlock on the door and kept the key. By law, evicting them would prove to be an uphill task due to the Rent Act.

Saintly intervention, however, saved the day. Like many Sindhi-speaking Hindus, this family had reverence for the Sufi tradition. They patronized a pir (a saint) of one of the many shrines around Dar-us-Salaam. After a spate of business losses, they consulted the pir.

'Leave the old lady's house right away,' instructed the saint.

To the Kingdom

Meanwhile, Majid decided to pursue another undergraduate degree in engineering, which his older brother, Abdul Basit, helped finance. After that, he got a job with Hindustan Machine Tools (HMT), a public sector enterprise that manufactured heavy equipment and later diversified into timepieces. He could have extended his engagement with HMT, but decided not to do so after the company asked him to sign an eight-year bond. He had already set his sights on migration.

Till 1979, he worked as a production engineer in two local companies. The same year, Basit completed a seven-year tenure as a medical officer in the Department of Atomic Energy's Nuclear Fuel Complex unit. Despite being a few marks shy of a passing grade for the United States Medical Licensing Examination, he had job offers from England and Australia. Instead, he opted for a job in the health ministry of a country that many Hyderabadis were flocking to, the Kingdom of Saudi Arabia (KSA).

That year, Abdul Basit sponsored his mother's Hajj visa to Saudi Arabia. This was a time when a woman could not perform Umrah and Hajj without a mehram (a family member with whom marriage is considered unlawful). My father accompanied his mother. It was during this trip in November 1979 that he decided to try his luck and find a job in the Kingdom.

But prior to leaving, Majid had been pursuing an opportunity with the Dhahran-based oil giant Arabian American Oil Company (ARAMCO). He remembered, 'I caught an advertisement for an engineering job in *The Times of India*. I further followed up on leads for this job via a manpower company in Mumbai.'

After his mother left Mecca to go back to Hyderabad, Majid remained in the holy city. On a phone call, his younger brother, Naeem, told him that he had received a telegram from ARAMCO asking him to select an interview date in Dhahran.

He ended up choosing a date in March. Not too long before leaving Mecca, he made a dua at the Kaaba—he wished for a job in Saudi. 'I thought to myself, if my dua is not accepted here, then perhaps something better is planned for me outside the Kingdom.'

At the time, he had two options—go back to Hyderabad and return in March for the ARAMCO interview or stay in the country and look for an opportunity in Jeddah.

The second option was risky. According to the Hajj visa rules back then, those undertaking the pilgrimage had to immediately head back to the airport for departure to their home countries. Jeddah was only about forty-five minutes away from Mecca, but the city was out of bounds for those on a Hajj visa. To move around and meet prospective employers, what Majid needed was a valid Azad visa.[6]

Doors Opening

For an Azad visa, a Saudi kafeel (employer or sponsor, usually a Saudi national) had to request the government for a single visa to hire someone for his organization. That visa was then sold to an agent, who, in turn, could sell that permit to someone seeking to enter Saudi Arabia for non-religious purposes. It was a coveted document for aspiring expatriates—with many willing to pay agents large sums of money to obtain the Azad visa and then job hunt in Saudi. Essentially, this was an unofficial, open-source visa of sorts.

Between Mecca and Jeddah, there were checkpoints where police officers would inspect documentation. Luckily, the Pakistani cab driver taking my father to Jeddah was familiar with a different route. He took the long route to Jeddah—through barren land—that helped them bypass the checkpoints.

'My elders told me not to pull such a stunt,' Majid told me many years later. 'But I did not have much luggage and my friend from Nizam College, Burhan Quadri, who was in Jeddah at that time, offered to let me stay with him.'

It was January 1980. Majid threw himself into job hunting as soon as he got to Jeddah. Quadri had a cousin who held a Canadian passport. He was an industrial engineer who referred him to another Hyderabadi named Hameed. Hameed, in turn, directed him towards an American Saudi Arabian Airlines employee named C.S. Davis.

When my father met Davis with a CV in hand, he said kindly, 'You are an engineer. Why do you want to work here? We decide ticket planning, airfare-related matters, and how many reservation houses are to be opened.'

The lead did not pan out as Majid had thought. He only had a week left on his Hajj visa.

Davis then directed him to a Lucknow native named Hyder who worked in the Department of Saudi Airlines Engine Planning. The helpful American knew that the aircraft maintenance department that Hyder headed needed a maintenance controller. Majid did not have prior aviation experience, but his mechanical engineering background came in handy. Getting into the Saudi Arabian Airlines's human resources building proved to be a hurdle too. Majid's physician brother had to pull some strings with a high-level contact in Saudi's Ministry of Health, who provided him access to the Saudi Airlines office.

Prayers Answered on Republic Day

On 26 January 1980, Majid entered the Saudi Airlines HR building. He was then taken to Hyder, who asked another Indian—a project manager—to take his interview. After a few basic questions, the manager addressed the elephant in the room.

'You do not have airline experience, nor have you ever handled parts of an aircraft,' he asserted.

Majid replied, 'All these parts are mechanical. I did study mechanical engineering after all.'

'Some parts are given more priority than others,' retorted the interviewer.

Majid answered, 'Well, there are books and manuals. You will guide me too.'

'Who has the time to explain all this to you?'

My father then asked the manager what his own qualifications were.

Irked by Majid's retorts and this specific response, the interviewer reeled off the names of all the institutions he had studied at. 'I am a Mussoorie-educated person with a BSc. I did my flight training with Rajiv Gandhi,' he replied.

It was at this point that Hyder interjected. 'He is an engineer. He'll figure it out.'

The project manager suggested that Majid take up the role of an air-conditioning engineer that would maybe pay more.

'Maybe, but I fly out next week,' said my father.

The project manager then relented by writing a letter to the HR department that read: 'He is a good, qualified candidate. But he lacks airline experience. If no seasoned candidates apply, hire him.'

Back in the 1970s and in the 1990s, when Saudization—the indigenizing of the work force—had not caught much steam, the mere names of companies like ARAMCO and Saudi Airlines had a certain sheen in the South Asian community. My father's job made him quite a prospect in the Hyderabadi marriage market. Two years after he started work in Saudi, he got married to my mother, who grew up in a Srinagar-based Hyderabadi family.

A Gateway to Many Different Worlds

Saudi Airlines had a gated community for its expatriate employees called Saudia City. The compound contained small villas, swimming pools, a grocery store and several playgrounds.

My sister and I look back on these years of our childhood as rather idyllic. The airline paid for our education up till the eighth grade in the American School, where my mother taught. We did not pick up our American twang in North America; we got our accent from all the Americana we were exposed to in school, the Saudia City compound and entertainment channels on television.

There were other perks with my father's job, including highly discounted air tickets on which we flew out to India twice a year, and later to North America as well. Living and playing around people of different nationalities helped us form a multicultural and utopian worldview. Our world was the school and the residential compound, which were a fifteen-minute drive apart.

To ensure that we would not become total Westerners, my parents spoke Dakhani at home and got a separate satellite TV subscription with India's newly minted Sony Entertainment Television and other Indian channels.

There were many foreigners like us who lived in such compounds. Here, expatriate women were not required to wear the abaya (a robe-like dress that women had to put on to cover themselves) and adhere to the conservative rules of the Kingdom. In Saudia City, everyone for the most part lived the same life. Hindus from Delhi, Catholics from Bombay and Punjabi-speaking Pakistanis from Lahore were among the families mine was close to.

A World beyond the Bubble

South Asians and North Americans of Saudi Arabian Airlines might have even lived and worked side by side. But there were differences when it came to remuneration. After all, the former were part of a group officially categorized as 'Third Country Nationals'; American and British expats fell in the more exalted 'First World National' category. It turned out that there existed a world outside out of Saudia City, which had a clear pecking order.

Indians, Pakistanis and Bangladeshis predominantly performed blue-collar jobs and were seen as lesser human beings. Even South Asians who held Western passports or lived the semi-charmed Saudi Airlines life were not exempt from racist attitudes of Saudis. That many of these lesser human beings were also fellow Muslims mattered little to the Kingdom's citizens and other Arab expatriates.

My realization of these social realities was accelerated after the World Trade Centre attack in September 2001. Many Western expatriates left the country in the wake of the tragedy. Gradually, schools and compounds became less multicultural due to expats leaving and local Saudis and other Arabs taking their place. Speaking Urdu or Hindi was enough for us to be condescendingly described as 'Bakistanis'.

To try and escape the second-class treatment, I would avoid speaking in Urdu. If I had not done this, perhaps I would have developed my penchant for Urdu earlier in life. Eventually, it took until my late twenties to seek out and start connecting with my roots.

From East to West to East

When I was growing up, what happened in India held little importance. If anyone had told me back in middle school that I would go on to build a career by writing about South Asian culture and develop an obsession with Urdu poetry as well literature, I would have scoffed. Maulana Azad and Nehru are among my political and literary heroes now, but it would be safe to say that I had not really heard of them until I was an adult. Telangana politics, which I think about a lot now, was nowhere near my radar—my sister and I had no idea about K. Chandrashekar Rao (KCR) or his party. The Nizam's name, Mir Osman Ali Khan, did not have any cultural significance for us.

The closest I would come to Hyderabadi culture in those days was the ghazal parties that my family would attend at the houses of certain relatives. My idea of Hyderabad was restricted to merely speaking Dakhani. Most of the time, I would have to be dragged to Hyderabadi and broader Indian associations parties both in and outside of Saudia City.

Back in Hyderabad, my first cousin's manje[7] in 1998 was the first time I remember having singers and comedians perform at a close extended family member's function. Throwing such parties was only possible because Aliya Begum's sons had made it big in the Gulf.

These parties would not have been complete without Makhdoom Mohiuddin's classic, *Ek Chameli Ke Mandve Tale*. I heard it at my cousin's manje for the first time but I was still a couple of decades away from understanding the role of Makhdoom and his work in Hyderabadi life.

After all, while growing up, Hyderabad was not my hometown. It just happened to be the native place of my parents.

My Own Ghar Wapsi of Sorts

I went to North America to study in the mid-2000s. The Telangana movement gained steam when I began working in the public affairs sector in Washington DC right out of college. The bandhs called by KCR or the loud calls for bifurcation were just white noise from the homeland. When I returned to Hyderabad in 2012 after a year of working in the US, the finer differences between Andhra Pradesh's two distinct Telugu communities were lost upon me. I was also unaware of the princely history that served as the backdrop of the struggle for statehood.

Working at an IT company and a social start-up incubator provided me with my first exposure to Indian life. I then took a year off, which allowed me the time to develop an interest in reading and writing. Immersing myself in English-language books written by Indian authors helped me make sense of the numerous contradictions, cultures and languages of the subcontinent.

While others like my sister, older relatives, high school as well as college friends were establishing their careers in North America, I decided to learn Urdu in Hyderabad instead. A workbook given to me by Khalid Saeed, a professor at MANUU, helped me learn the nastaleeq Urdu script.

Before going to the School of Oriental and African Studies (SOAS), University of London for a master's in South Asian Area Studies, I spent a few months in Washington DC and Toronto. Under Lahore-born journalist Raza Rumi's encouragement, I began trying my hand at writing about South Asian security and culture. My grad school experience in London allowed me to dive deeper into the history and culture of the subcontinent.

I returned to Hyderabad in 2017. A year later, the weekly magazine of a business newspaper published my long-form article on the 70th anniversary of Police Action. Since then, Urdu literature and my freelance writing for various publications have enabled me to reconnect with my Hyderabadi, Indian and overall South Asian heritage that had once never fully resonated with me.

Before Covid-19 hit, I joined Siasat.com, the online English edition of the Urdu daily founded by Abid Ali Khan (Chapter 1) and Mehboob Hussain Jigar. That's where my second mentor, Mir Ayoob Ali Khan, (Chapter 5) helped hone my understanding of Hyderabad's history and heritage. I forged connections with Telugu-speaking Hyderabadis and Kayasthas whose families have been settled in Hyderabad city for several generations. Now, after all these years, I can truly say that Hyderabad feels like home.

But a trip back to what once felt like a home had me thinking about whether Saudi Arabia will continue to figure heavily in the lives of Hyderabadis.

Time to Look Beyond Saudi Arabia?

When one door closed for Hyderabadi Muslims in 1948, about two decades later another opened in the Gulf. Between the 1980s and 2000s, if anyone visited a Muslim household in Hyderabad city, chances were that at least one member of the family would be making their living in the Middle East.

As labourers, drivers, customer salesmen, air-conditioner mechanics or engineers, Hyderabadis still kept their heads down no matter the exploitation or the unfair treatment meted out to them. Of course, South Asians with American, Canadian, European and Australian passports had the economic and institutional benefits of being citizens of these countries. Still, to some Saudis, the passport did not always affect their perception towards these 'lesser' subjects.

Hyderabadis had no choice but to rise above this prejudice. If they did not do that, their households back home would have to suffer the financial consequences of it.

Today, jobs for foreigners in Saudi are not as abundant as they were between the 1970s and the early 2010s. Mohammed Bin Salman's economic and cultural overhaul of the Kingdom has seen many Hyderabadis returning to India, especially with the young Crown Prince disincentivizing the hiring of non-Saudis.[8]

News of the customer service executive, cash counter supervisor, general supervisor positions at food stores and supermarkets being reserved for the local Saudi population[9] had me asking myself the following question: What could Saudization mean for Indian expats?

A five-day trip to Jeddah in early 2024 would give me a clearer answer—one that concerns Hyderabadis whose livelihoods, real estate ventures, extravagant weddings or children's college educations have been bankrolled by Saudi riyals.

After seeing so many more local, non-Saudi men as well as women working at fast-food restaurants and retail outlets, the true magnitude of the change in Saudi dawned on me. But a more telling incident occurred before boarding a bullet train to Madina from Jeddah's Sulaymaniyah train station. I would have never imagined that a native Arab would actively and courteously assist a South Asian trying to find their way around.

The Kingdom is not the cash cow it once was for Hyderabadis, Indians and South Asians. Any Hyderabadi looking to take the same path my father did to earn in Saudi Arabia, will have to rethink such a plan as quotas to hire more Saudi nationals in engineering jobs are being implemented.[10]

Regardless of what all these changes mean for Hyderabadis, the Kingdom of Saudi Arabia is itself a character in the comeback story of Hyderabadi Muslims post-1948. The educational privileges and material comforts that my generation enjoys today is a direct result of those who left their homes and toiled in the Kingdom. The economic power that came about because of Gulf money has also made it possible for us to take the othering happening in present-day India somewhat in our stride.

Mohiuddin Qadri Zor and A.Q. Sarwari: *Urdu Hai Jis Ka Naam*

Co-authored with Dr Zamir Ahmad Butt

اردو ہے جس کا نام ہمیں جانتے ہیں داغ

ہندوستاں میں دھوم ہماری زباں کی ہے

—داغ دہلوی

Urdu hai jis ka naam humeen jaante hai Daagh
Hindustan mein dhoom humari zabaan ki hai

Daagh, we know, the language that has Urdu as its name
Celebrated across India is its fame

—Daagh Dehlvi

Hyderabad's Imprints on Kashmir

On a summer morning in Kashmir, the Dal Lake of Srinagar shimmers with the reflection of the Hazratbal Dargah (shrine), a structure that houses a strand of the Prophet's hair. The Pir Panjal mountains frame this tranquil scene. Although the searing Deccan heat of Hyderabad feels so far away from the toasty sunlight of the morning at the shrine, Zamir Ahmad Butt, a native Kashmiri who obtained his PhD from the University of Hyderabad, and I are thinking of a connection between the two cities.

In 1953, Bakshi Ghulam Mohammad, the new Prime Minister of Jammu and Kashmir, began inviting professionals from mainland India to work in the bureaucratic, academic and other sectors. Among them was Hyder Siddiqui, an architect and native of Hyderabad. He was invited to Srinagar to spearhead the design and construction of a lot of new government buildings. Along with Siddiqui came other architects from his hometown, one of them being my grandfather, Syed Rahim.

My mother grew up in Kashmir, but my connection to the Valley is a limited one at best. But this time, I was here to learn more about two Hyderabadis whose names have become inseparable from the story of Urdu in Kashmir.

Upon leaving the shrine and traversing west on Hazratbal Road, the calmness gets exchanged for the hustle and bustle of the University Main Road. Sir Syed Gate, the main entrance to the University of Kashmir, is a five-minute walk away.

Inside the Urdu department's building on the sprawling campus, Zamir and I came across a huge board with the names of the PhD awardees from the department. The list also included the names of their supervisors. One of the names in the supervisor column was of a man that Vehshi Saeed, a renowned short-story writer, also referred to as 'Kashmir's Imam-e-Urdu'—Professor Abdul Qadir Sarwari.

The 'Imam-e-Urdu' played a major role in the development of scholarship and budding literary talent at the university's Urdu department. But the pioneer of this department was also a true-blue Hyderabadi. He had his moniker too: Baba-e-Deccaniyat, the father of Deccan studies. His name was Mohiuddin Qadri Zor.

An Urdu Prodigy

Born in the Old City's Shahgunj area to Syed Ghulam Shah Qadri and Basheer-un-Nissa in 1905, Mohiuddin Qadri Zor would soon follow in the footsteps of his maternal grandfather Anwarullah Khan, a renowned scholar and the founder of Jamia Nizamia, Hyderabad's most well-known theological seminary.

At the age of four, he began his schooling at the Kayastha Pathshala in the Baragalli part of Hussaini Alam. He continued his studies in the Brahmo-Khatri-founded Mufeed-ul-Anam Boys High School, after which he completed his intermediate education at City College. He then attended the Jamia Nizamia seminary.

A young Mohiuddin would continue to wear this badge of academic excellence well into his undergraduate years at Osmania University. Even before he completed his MA in linguistic studies from OU, he had already authored a few books. One of these, titled *Teen Shayar* (Three Poets), was a comparative analysis of the works of three poets: Mir Taqi Mir, Mir Anees and Horace Smith. After finishing the MA in 1927, the Hyderabad government sent him to England for his doctorate. In London, Zor obtained degrees in phonetics from both University College London (UCL) and SOAS.

His research in London revolved around the inception and evolution of Urdu. Ralph Liley Turner, eminent Indologist and his supervisor at SOAS, believed that Zor's research provided the foundation of Urdu's comparative history.[1]

Studying Urdu through the lens of contemporary linguistics was also new, which is why Zor undertook more research on phonetics in Paris.[2] According to him, Urdu did not just remain confined to Punjab after Mahmood Ghaznavi's conquest of that region. But it also spread to the North-West Frontier Province and Allahabad.[3] This line of thought expanded on scholar Hafiz Mehmood Khan Sherani's theory that Urdu originated in Punjab.[4] Contrary to many other scholars' conclusions, Zor asserted that Urdu and Hindi could not have originated from Khari Boli and Braj Bhasha.[5]

When Zor returned to Hyderabad, he joined OU's Urdu department as a reader.

Baba-e-Deccaniyat

In the Panjagutta area of Hyderabad, an old building with Moorish elements flanks the New Age metro station of Irrum Manzil. This building houses the Idara-e-Adabiyat-e-Urdu (IAU), a prestigious Hyderabadi institution to which scholars from all over the world still flock to.

Here is where Zamir and I met Rafi Zor, the seventy-five-year-old son of Mohiuddin Qadri Zor. Rafi is the director of IAU, which was co-founded by his father in 1931.

In the IAU premises, portraits of Jigar Moradabadi, Firaq Gorakhpuri and other Urdu luminaries cast their gaze upon students perfecting their calligraphic strokes. As these young calligraphers in the making do so under the supervision of master penman Mohammed Abdul Ghaffar who has been teaching since 1997, Rafi Zor took us back to the Hyderabad of the late nineteenth century. 'Urdu had replaced Persian as the government language in 1884,' Rafi elaborated, 'Mahbub Ali Khan, the sixth Nizam, patronized poets from the north. Some of these versifiers were Daagh Dehlvi and Ameer Minai.' Such was the value of the language in those days. Rafi told us that simply reading and writing Urdu was not enough to land a government job. Elegance was of the essence. 'Even a policeman or army soldier was required to wield a "qalam"—a pen—with finesse before he could brandish a firearm,'[6] he added.

The publication of Altaf Hussain Hali's *Muqqadama-e-Sher-o-Shayari* in 1893 was a seminal event in the world of Urdu letters.[7] The treatise is said to have introduced the genre of criticism in modern

Urdu.[8] It lambasted the Lucknow-based poets for privileging romantic content over moral values and national feelings.[9]

Hali's influence spanned across decades. In 1925, when Zor was twenty, he wrote a book that introduced the students of OU to the art of literary critique. *Rooh-e-Tanqeed* contained the precocious author's well-formed thoughts about styles, genres and entire schools of thought. *Hindustani Lasaaneeyaat* (Indian Linguistics) and *Urdu Shahpaare* (Urdu Masterpieces) are still fixtures in Urdu and other linguistic educational programmes throughout India. In 1940, he compiled the complete works of Hyderabad city's founder Muhammad Quli Qutub Shah, who was known to be the first Urdu poet to have a collection of poems to his name.

Zor's versatility also extended to historical prose. His *Sair-e-Golconda* is a hark back to the Qutub Shahi years of the late sixteenth and seventeenth centuries, containing tales about the establishment of the Mecca Masjid in Hyderabad and the influence of Hayat Bakshi Begum during the reign of her son Abdullah Qutub Shah.

Back to Hyderabad

In 1931, Zor founded the IAU along with Abdul Majeed Siddiqi, Abdul Qadeer Siddiqi, Naseeruddin Hashmi and Abdul Qadir Sarwari.[10]

This institute, which first operated out of Zor's bedroom, was established to promote Urdu scholarship and preserve the literature of the Deccan. Compiling as well as cataloguing manuscripts and other treasures that date back all the way to the Bahmani Sultanate of the thirteenth century was no small task. On top of that, IAU was also a calligraphy learning centre from the start. The expansive premises of his house, Tahneeyat Manzil, hosted an all-India level calligraphy competition in 1942.

By 1945, Zor had been promoted to the post of professor. Soon, he would go on to head the Urdu department at OU and become the dean of its Faculty of Arts and Oriental Studies.

He had grand plans for IAU. To put them into action, he purchased land around the Katora Hauz area close to the Golconda fort. His mission was supported by Osman Ali Khan, the seventh Nizam, who had inherited his father's keen interest in promoting Urdu. The Nizam allotted four acres of the Sarf-e-Khas—crown lands belonging to the Asaf Jahi family—for Professor Zor and his companions to construct a bigger home for IAU.

But there was trouble brewing on the horizon for the princely state and its ruling regime whose support was essential for this endeavour.

This storm of Police Action, which occurred while Professor Zor was principal of Dar-ul-Uloom College, would merely delay and not derail his ambitions.

'Joo-e-Sheer'

In a matter-of-fact tone that reminded me of Halima Bi, (Chapter 2), Rafi told us about how Police Action had affected his father. 'He wept for three straight days and could not eat anything,' Rafi recalled. The IAU director also added, 'With the Asaf Jahi establishment deposed, the Nizam's government would no longer be able to provide the support and lands it had promised for Idara.'

Professor Zor then appealed to an aristocrat from Barkatpura, but the nobleman was unwilling to part with even a small corner of his estate for IAU. Understandably, Baba-e-Deccaniyat got the same reaction from other nobles whose assistance he sought. These feudal lords had fallen on tough times after Police Action. Their landed income had dwindled massively, and they had been reduced to selling their expensive heirlooms and possessions for cash. For many of them, there was no question of granting land to a cultural institution, considering that they were selling their palatial deodhis (mansions) at large discounts.

In a MANUU mini-documentary, the late reporter Aijaz Qureshi poetically notes that acquiring land in those days was joo-e-sheer, which translates to 'a stream of milk' and metaphorically means an impossible task. The idiom is also used to refer to something precious that one struggles to attain.

Eventually, it was one of Professor Zor's own who came through for IAU. His wife Tahneeyat-un-Nisa Begum, the daughter of prominent noble and educationist Rafat Yar Jung II, allotted some of her land for the building. Ultimately, the building took five years to construct.

Divided into departments of language, critique, translation, poets and writers, science, women's studies, children and examinations, IAU finally had a newer, more expansive home in 1960. Police Action might have temporarily impeded Professor Zor's plans to find a bigger home for IAU, but he continued to flourish in his professional career, taking up important positions such as the head of the Urdu department of OU and as the principal of Chaderghat Government Degree College.

It was not smooth sailing for IAU even after that. 'After the building's construction, Idara had a budget of Rs 25,000 in mind,' Rafi told us. 'The Rs 25,000 from Maulana Azad helped but it was not enough to keep many of the programs running,' he also disclosed.

In December 1960, Professor Zor decided to retire from academia in Hyderabad. But about a year later, he would come across the man who would become one of IAU's largest benefactors.

Bakshi Ghulam Mohammad

When it came to deciding the guest of honour to inaugurate IAU in 1961, the options were Prime Minister Jawaharlal Nehru, who waxed as lyrically in Urdu as he did in English, and Bakshi Ghulam Mohammad, the Prime Minister of Jammu and Kashmir. Nehru had already inaugurated Urdu Hall, an Urdu-medium college and cultural venue that many high-profile litterateurs would visit whenever they came to Hyderabad. A poet and writer from Uttar Pradesh suggested that Zor invite Bakshi, a potential benefactor, to inaugurate IAU.

Sheikh Abdullah's successor may have had a checkered legacy with his brutal repression of popular and political dissent,[11] but he had an eye for capable individuals. Bakshi recognized that the man at the helm of IAU would make for an excellent dean of faculty and Urdu department head at the University of Kashmir. The Jammu and Kashmir PM then asked Baba-e-Deccaniyat if he was up to the task.

Being a person who loved every particle of his native land, Professor Zor required some convincing before he would venture far away from home to add more accolades to an already storied career.

The scholar at the helm of Idara was being asked to move to Kashmir at a particularly difficult moment for Urdu in Hyderabad. In 1950, OU had shed its identity as an Urdu-medium university and instead taken on an English one. Official government gazette notifications that were once issued in Urdu were now being disseminated in English.[12]

Professor Zor finally agreed to take the position, but not before setting some conditions, one of which was having a free hand to make appointments. In March 1961, only a few days after the inauguration of IAU, he set off for Kashmir.

A Mentor to Kashmiris

Professor Zor briefly carried out his duties as a dean at the beginning of his one-and-a-half-year stint at the University of Kashmir, but his effort in developing the Urdu scholarship and literary talent was what made his brief time there special.

Mushtaq Haider, an assistant professor in University of Kashmir's Urdu department, pointed out, 'Like Dakhani Urdu, Kashmiri Urdu contains local influences that makes it sound different from the proper Urdu spoken in Uttar Pradesh and Delhi. People in our department speak proper Urdu because of Dr Zor and Dr Sarwari. They taught their students real Urdu, who then taught us.'

Zor was known for propping up talented pupils who were looking to be published. Not only did he impart knowledge to those he taught, but he showcased their literary talents even when they were unknown entities. In the prologue of his short-story collection *Barf Mein Aag* (Ice on Fire), Hamidi Kashmiri acknowledged how IAU provided a bigger platform for the works of Kashmiri writers and poets through its magazine *Sab-Ras*.[13]

Professor Zor had a knack for spotting and nurturing talented poets and writers. One of them was Farooq Nazki, who was a literary assistant at the Jammu and Kashmir Academy of Cultures, Arts and Languages in the early 1960s. Later, he would go on to become the director of Doordarshan as well as All India Radio in Srinagar. After Zor heard Nazki's radio programme called *Khermun*, he asked him to pursue his MA in Urdu because they needed competent teachers at the university. Nazki resigned from his literary assistant job the next day to join the MA programme.

'I became one of his favourite students,' Nazki remembered warmly, 'He told me that my poetry had the khushboo—the aroma— of Faiz.' Nazki's mentor then asked him to compose an essay on Faiz for *Sab-Ras*. 'He wrote a personal note to me after reading my essay which read, "Your writing is good enough to be published, but while writing the letter '*seen* (س),' you make three curves. You need not make these curves."'

At first, Nazki thought it was a very minuscule error, but, later on, he grew thankful for his mentor's constructive criticism and his attention to detail. 'In his brief tenure, he encouraged a lot of young and unknown writers. Unfortunately, his time there ended up being very brief,' commented Nazki.

Baba-e-Deccaniyat's time in Kashmir was not without hiccups though. For instance, Rashid Bakshi, brother of Ghulam, had tried to strong-arm Zor into appointing a crony at the university.

'*Main kisi ki sifaarish nahin manta* (I do not give weight to anybody's influence),' he asserted.

This rebuff courted the wrath of Rashid, who was known to have a coercive streak. He tried to turn the university's staff against the person who dared to defy Rashid Bakshi's diktat. When Professor Zor retaliated, it was in lyrical fashion at an all-India mushaira that Bakshi Ghulam Mohammad presided over in Srinagar. Making eye contact with the PM whose brother had tried to intimidate him, Zor recited:

> *Hum ghareebon pe ameero ki khudaai chalti*
> *Baais-e-barhami bazm-e-butaan hai kuch log*

> The rich man's lordship always hovers over the poor's existence
> One is the idol of a congregation, the other is the cause of vexation

The Best-Laid Plans of Mice and Men

Professor Zor also began learning the Kashmiri language. Considering his flair for languages, it would have only been a few years before he became fluent.

But on 24 September 1962, death prevented a linguistic immersion into Kashmiri soil short. He was given a funeral with full state honours before being buried at Khanyar Sharif. The Jammu and Kashmir government declared a holiday on that day. Farooq Nazki put it quite poetically.

'*Unn ki umar ne unn ke saath wafadari nahin ki* (His age was not exactly loyal to him).'

According to Nazki, Srinagar was also on its way to becoming a second centre of Urdu after Hyderabad for Professor Zor. Beyond publishing the work of talented Kashmiri writers, the Hyderabadi Urdu stalwart, for whom the Valley became a second home, also planned to transform IAU into a full-fledged university.

Baba-e-Deccaniyat's death left the University of Kashmir's students without a guiding hand. However, it would not be long before the void would be filled by another one of IAU's co-founders.

Imam-e-Urdu

Abdul Qadir Sarwari was born on 19 August 1906 in Hyderabad into a modest family. He earned an LLB and an MA in Urdu from OU where he also became a lecturer in 1929. He later went on to head the Urdu department at Mysore University. In 1948, he returned to his alma mater OU, where he took up the same post. Like Zor, he also served as the principal of Chaderghat College.

Professor Sarwari moved to Kashmir in 1963, the year after Zor's death. Zamir and I heard about his life story from Vasiq, one of his California-based sons. We met him during one of his visits to Hyderabad.

I was also pleasantly surprised to learn from him that the Sarwaris were neighbours of my maternal family in Srinagar's Jawahar Nagar locality. Like my mother, Vasiq's younger sister, Nikhat, also went to Presentation Convent, and he received the same boys' convent education like my maternal uncle.

Those were different times in the Kashmir Valley, Vasiq told us. 'I saw the Beatles there. That is the way life was,' he remembered. But the region had already started to become marked by armed conflict. The Sarwari family was in the thick of the 1965 war between India and Pakistan.

That full-scale conflict saw an irregular tribal army infiltrate the Valley from Pakistan through Operation Gibraltar. Once the infiltrators provoked a response, Operation Grand Slam was put into action. This had the Pakistan Army open fire on another front, with the objective of capturing the Akhnoor Bridge in Jammu. Seizing that bridge would sever the only road link between India and Kashmir.[14]

Vasiq mentioned that those in Kashmir would have become Pakistanis overnight had Operation Gibraltar and Operation Grand Slam succeeded. 'A lot of homes in Jawahar Nagar were hit by stray bullets. We had no idea what to expect. All we could do was just see how the situation played out.'

The Indian Army was able to fend off the infiltrators in order to keep the Pakistani Army at bay.

Inheriting the Mantle

At the Shahenshah Palace Hotel in Dal Gate, Zamir met Vehshi Saeed, a former student of Professor Sarwari. Speaking in Kashmiri-accented Urdu, Saeed spoke of a learned but understated personality.

'He sometimes had the look of an old-school Urdu scholar with the sherwani (a long-sleeved close-fitting knee-length coat with a stand-up collar worn by men) and topi (a type of formal hat). Yet, never did he make anyone feel that he was so educated, learned and has a lot of knowledge about literature. Kashmiris owe him a lot.'

Although a true-blue Hyderabadi, Professor Sarwari's Urdu was devoid of the pronunciations or colloquial slang that the Dakhani dialect is known for. Of course, he used to use the kh (خ) rather than q (ق) when pronouncing certain words as most Hyderabadis do.

Sarwari picked up from where Zor had left off. Just two years after Saeed enrolled in the university's Urdu department, Sarwari read his short story *Jamhooreeyat ka Janaza* (The Funeral of Democracy) in the Bombay-based magazine *Shayar*. Saeed was just starting out then, so he was grateful when his mentor recommended the story to Professor Hamidi Kashmiri, another prominent educator at the Urdu department.

'He asked Hamidi to get his students to analyse the story,' Saeed told Zamir.

Professor Sarwari's protégé continued, '"Look at how excellently he ended the story," that is what he told Professor Hamidi.'

In his monumental work *Kashmir Mein Urdu* (Urdu in Kashmir), which chronicles the 250-year-old journey of the language in the Valley, Sarwari predicted that his protégé Saeed would make it big in the literary world.

His faith was not misplaced. Saeed, now seventy-eight years old, has since gone on to publish many works like the novella *Maazi aur Haal* (Past and Present), as well as short-story collections like *Khwaab Haqeeqat* (Dream, Reality) and a novel *Patthar Patthar Aaina* (Mirrors Among Rocks).

The Chronicler of Urdu in Kashmir

Zamir also spoke about Professor Sarwari with another one of his accomplished protégés, Mohammad Yousuf Taing. Zamir met Taing at his home in Rawalpora. The biographer of Sheikh Abdullah sat on a sofa in a living room that was decorated with several awards and photographs of himself with literary luminaries, including Faiz Ahmed Faiz.

'Without *Kashmir Mein Urdu*, an authoritative history of Urdu in my homeland would not exist,' informed Taing. While at the Academy of Cultures, Arts and Languages, Taing came across a manuscript of this work. As an editor of the mammoth, three-volume magnum opus, Taing witnessed first-hand how much blood and sweat had been put into this book by Sarwari.

Professor Sarwari died in 1971, and the volumes were posthumously published. The first volume looks at how Urdu came to Kashmir before Maharaja Pratap Singh made it the government language in 1889. The second volume covers the anti-Dogra movements in Kashmir and the broader Indian struggle for freedom. It also looks at how literary trends were playing out in the midst of this political turmoil. In the third volume, Professor Sarwari mentions some of his students whom he thought to be the future of Urdu literature in Kashmir. One of them was Farooq Nazki, who told us how thrilled he was to see his poems published in *Kashmir Mein Urdu*.

'Padhe Farsi, Beche Tel'

Back in Hyderabad, Vasiq Sarwari told us how much his father loved his work. 'He gave his life for linguistics before he died in 1971,' he emphasized.

Like Zor, he hoped to be laid to rest in his native soil, but he was buried in Kashmir. Although the last name Sarwari suggests that he was of Afghan ancestry, Taing believed that his forefathers were from Kashmir. Yusuf Taing felt that given Sarwari's ancestry, it was God's will that he be buried in the Valley. His resting place can be found in the Jawahar Nagar locality that he once lived in.

Only one of Professor Sarwari's children, Zubeida, would take to linguistics and carry on his legacy. After obtaining a PhD in Arabic from OU, she taught at Women's College and passed away in Hyderabad, where her second son still lives. Her only daughter who still lives in Hyderabad is a retired professor.

Vasiq told us that his father wanted to keep him and his siblings away from the arts. Like many Indians in the 1970s and 1980s, Vasiq studied engineering, with the knowledge that it would improve his prospects to move abroad.

He landed in New Jersey, where his brother, Junaid, lived, in August 1975. After completing a master's in industrial engineering and logistics, he worked as a staff engineer for ShopRite, a grocery supermarket chain in New Jersey. His move further west began with a stint of a year-and-a-half in Boise, Idaho. Finally, he settled down in a suburb of Los Angeles.

Vasiq loves to travel but he was honest about not having much of a connection with the city of his birth. 'All of us cut the cord with Hyderabad in the 1980s,' he said about himself and his siblings.

Junaid now lives in tropical Orlando, Florida. Another one of his siblings, Fazal, lives in a suburb of Chicago, a hub for Hyderabadis. The youngest sibling, Nikhat, lives in Long Island. Rifat Sarwari, who had moved to New Jersey in 1996, is no more.

Vasiq does not have children. When I enquired if any of his nieces and nephews speak, read and write Urdu, he informed, 'Not really. Pretty much everybody is focused on engineering or medicine.'

This was relatable. Almost all of my own maternal cousins identify more with North America than India; most of them are in engineering or medicine-related fields. Aside from relishing biryani, khatti daal (Hyderabad's take on daal, tamarind flavoured red lentils), tamatar ki chutney (bitter tomato curry with fried chillies) and other household staples, the Deccan culture does not figure heavily in their lives.

They do not see Hyderabad as their homeland. Most of them do not have any sort of identity crisis, nor do they feel sentimental about their roots. Quite simply, they see Hyderabad as the place that parents and grandparents came from.

We do not need to travel all the way to North America to get a sense that Urdu no longer occupies the central piece it used to in the life of the Deccan. It is often seen as an exotic pleasure of the affluent. The language is taught in religious schools, but there is an all-pervasive sense that it is a relic of the past, out of step with the demands and needs of modern education and employment. Hence the saying, '*Padhe Farsi, bechein tel* (The only thing you can do with Persian is sell oil).' Now, one can perhaps replace Persian with Urdu in the idiom.

Urdu in Today's Hyderabad

The year 1956 is seen as a watershed for the fall of Urdu in Hyderabad. Though as early as 1952, the central government had already been ratcheting up the pressure to eliminate the use of Urdu in courts.[15] The dilution had already commenced with the introduction of Telugu as a language of the courts much before the linguistic division of the state.

Until the 1970s, cultural organizations and artists' guilds valiantly held the fort for Urdu. One of the ways they did this was by frequently hosting mushairas in Hyderabad city. But the writing was on the wall—only English would pay the bills. As of 2012, only fourteen of the 1,800 private schools in Hyderabad district are Urdu-medium.[16]

In 2017, then Chief Minister KCR announced that Urdu would become the second language of the government. Although his regime's inability-cum-unwillingness to appoint teachers or even provide certain amenities to schools did not go unnoticed.[17]

There has been a resurgence in interest in the language during more recent years. It has been fuelled by festivals graced by Bollywood stars, 'anjumans' where one can learn poetry without engaging with the script and snazzily edited social media clips that feature eloquent recitations of Ghalib. But this interest is somewhat cosmetic, for it has neither translated into increased funding for research institutes nor more footfalls for the traditional Urdu press. It is Urdu for the social media age, and it does not quite encourage the depth and temperament required to produce work of the quality that Zor and Sarwari popularized back in their day.

Having said all this, there is more to the story of Urdu's decline in Hyderabad than government neglect or the rise of social media.

Hyderabad's Fragmented Urdu World

Egos and power struggles have played a role in the erosion of Hyderabad's Urdu landscape. The Fine Arts Academy is an artists' guild that emerged in the 1950s. Older Hyderabadis still remember the academy, especially its humour poetry wing Zinda Dillan-e-Hyderabad, as a fountainhead of Urdu talent.

But Zinda Dillan split from the Academy in the 1970s, precipitating a battle between those who claim it is still part of the Fine Arts Academy and those who wish for Zinda Dillan to remain a separate entity. Half a century on, the fault lines still run deep, no less because of the Urdu fraternity's tendency to hold on to grudges and indulge in power struggles.[18]

The internal politics have chipped away at the collaborative spirit that once prevailed in Hyderabad. Talent began to be either held back or promoted based on factions and personal grudges.

After Police Action, it was the humour poets of Hyderabad who brought some cheer to a scarred city. In the 1950s and 1960s, Hyderabad was the humour poetry capital of the subcontinent. The situation is rather different now—one estimate suggests that there are only six practicing humour poets in the city today. As to what extent this grim scenario can be attributed to lack of government patronage to Urdu post-1948 or petty squabbles of litterateurs who failed to nurture talent pools outside their coteries, that is a matter of perspective.

Though after everything I have come to learn about Abdul Qadir Sarwari's passion for teaching and Mohiuddin Qadri Zor's willingness to open doors for protégés, the partisanship in the Urdu landscape feels like a devolution. This is clearly why Rafi Zor made the following lament to both Zamir and I: '*Ab woh jazba aur khuloos nahin raha logon mein jo pehle tha* (People do not possess the drive and sincerity from the old days anymore).'

Mir Ayoob Ali Khan: Nurturing the Pen and Tablet

ہم پرورشِ لوح و قلم کرتے رہیں گے
دل پہ جو گزرتی ہے رقم کرتے رہیں گے
— فیض احمد فیض

Hum parvarish-e-lauh-o-qalam karte rahenge
Dil pe jo guzarti hai raqam karte rahenge

By nurturing the pen and tablet, we play our part
In writing about the travails of the heart

—Faiz Ahmed Faiz

Banjara Hills Road Number 12: A Bastion of Hyderabad's History

The Palladian-style building of the Virinchi Hospital looms over the chaotic signal and traffic on Road Number 1 in the Banjara Hills locality. At Virinchi's front entrance, the hospital name is written in

English, Urdu and Telugu scripts. For some, this may come across as a sign of the city's tolerant, cosmopolitan ethos.

However, the same ethos could not be found in the hospital's chairperson Madhavi Latha as she campaigned to dethrone AIMIM chief Asaduddin Owaisi from his parliamentary constituency. In an interview on the popular TV show *Aap Ki Adalat,* during her Lok Sabha campaign on a BJP ticket, Latha accused her opponent of planning to contest the election on issues like the beef ban and the Ayodhya dispute. One rhetorical question even harked back to the past.[1] She asked if Owaisi's 'plan was to establish an "Osmanistan"'. This was a reference to the independent Nizam-ruled state that Qasim Razvi's MIM envisioned during the 1940s.

Across Virinchi Hospital is a long road that is, in many ways, a capsule of Hyderabad's history. Road Number 12 is home to people like Oudesh Rani Bawa (Chapter 9) and Burgula Narsing Rao, keepers of some of the most fascinating anecdotes, books and other material about the city's past, present and future. Road Number 12 also hosts the residence of Ayoob Ali Khan, who has played a key role in the English journalism landscape of Hyderabad.

The late Vara Lakshmi Sarvadevabhatla, an Urdu–Telugu bilingual writer and participant of the Telangana Peasants' Rebellion, admitted that journalists had failed to accurately capture the upheaval and trials of those who experienced the Police Action. To her, Telugu and Urdu litterateurs did a better job of capturing it through their prose.[2]

Post-1948, Urdu newspapers were under attack with outlets like *Rehbar-e-Deccan, Meezan* and *Nizam Gazette* vehemently adopting a pro-Independence, anti-India stance before Police Action. Abid Ali Khan (Chapter 2) and Mehboob Hussain Jigar founded *Siasat* so that it could serve as a bridge between Urdu journalism in Hyderabad and the Indian Union. The English outlets were not interested in the Deccan's pre-1948 history, nor did they set much store by stories concerning the Muslim population of Hyderabad.

It would take almost half a century for that attitude to change. The transformation only began when Mir Ayoob Ali Khan returned to the city in 1998, after seventeen years of working at the *Saudi Gazette* in Jeddah.

Serish Nanisetti, bureau chief for Hyderabad at *The Hindu*, told me that Khan brought a 'certain kind of tolerance back to journalism in Hyderabad'. By doing so, he opened the door for a kind of cultural reportage that helped communities understand each other's pasts and honour their common heritage.

A Much-Needed Dose of Tolerance

Serish was working as a features editor at *Deccan Chronicle* (DC) when he first heard of Khan. At that time, A.T. Jayanti, the chief editor of the English edition, was looking for talented writers from the city.

'Hyderabad is a strange place,' Serish revealed, 'it is home to two journalism colleges, but we have very few local journalists from here. Even today, people from outside the city mostly fill that void.'

Even though he had been away from his hometown for two decades, Khan's connection with the city was enduring. His insider perspective was an asset for DC and later to *The Times of India*. To illustrate what Khan brought to the table, Serish told me about a story that the then Saudi-returned journalist pitched on the opening of the Nizam's Museum. The museum showcased the gifts, souvenirs and mementos that Mir Osman Ali Khan had received to celebrate his silver jubilee as Hyderabad's ruler.

'Ayoob Sahaab told Jayanti, "I am going to do this story. Imagine all the Nizam's gifts being displayed in a city that only has one museum,"' recounted Serish, who is also the author of *Golconda/Bagnagar/ Hyderabad: The Rise and Fall of a Global Metropolis in Medieval India*. Ayoob's story did not need much editing, Serish remembered. Reader feedback suggested that it had struck a chord.

In the decades following Police Action, Serish said that the royalty and nobility had become somewhat disconnected from the city and its life. Stories on the 'City' pages of the newspapers were missing a historical and social context, the kind that is developed only by engaging deeply with the surroundings.

'For example, if I choose to write about the Golconda area, I can do so in two ways,' Serish explained. 'The first way will have me pushing for encroachments in Golconda to be removed. I can do that only if I am not from this area and I do not know the Golconda Fort. The second way is by getting to know the Golconda area and the people who live there. When I do that, I might not propose this solution.'

Ayoob Ali Khan was an insider. His parents had witnessed the horrors of the Razakars and the Police Action in rural Telangana. Their lives had been entirely overturned by those times. I had heard some of the anecdotes of those days from him, when used to be my boss at Siasat.com, the English web-only edition of *Siasat*. Now, I wanted to dig deeper to trace the arc of his life.

I went to see Ayoob at his residence, in a by-lane off Road Number 12. In his living room, I spotted a photograph of him shaking hands with Abdullah bin Abdulaziz, then Crown Prince of Saudi Arabia. We then started by talking about his family.

Mansabdars of Telangana

Ayoob Ali Khan's lineage is one of privilege. His father Mir Vazeeruddin Ali Khan (also known as Ishaq Miyan) was a mansabdar who was given lands by the Nizam in return for military services. His paternal grandmother was also from a family whose members received lands for such services. Her family lived on that land with other Syeds, who claimed to be descendants of the Prophet.

Ayoob's father Vazeer might have lacked a formal English education. But with a job in the Mehkama-e-Aabkari (excise department) in

Hyderabad city and lands in Chilkepalli village (15 kilometres from Zaheerabad) he really did not feel the need for an advanced degree.

Ayoob's mother came from a landed family that belonged to the Bilalpur village, also about 20 kilometres from Zaheerabad. Born as Sughra Bi, she was the fifth among four girls and five brothers. Considering the similar backgrounds and the Syed lineage, she got married to Vazeer. After marriage, her name was changed to Amena.

Unlike many Hyderabadis from feudal backgrounds, Ayoob does not shy away from elaborating on the dark side of the strata. The bonded labourers that used to work the fields were totally subservient to the aristocrats.

'It was common for aristocratic men to sleep around with lower-caste women,' Ayoob stated. 'These women were pejoratively referred to as dhernis,' he deplored further.

Amena stood out in this highly stratified society, where upper-class women were expected to be confined to the house and run domestic matters. 'People got scared whenever she used to ride off from the house on a horse. No one would have any idea as to when she would return home,' Ayoob elaborated.

It was a comfortable life in Chilkepalli, not lacking in anything. But things would drastically change from September 1948.

Kohir: Contagious to Northeast Karnataka

Today, Chilkepalli, Zaheerabad and Kohir are part of the Sangareddy district. But in 1948, they came under the Medak district. The latter district saw a lot of looting and destruction of Muslim property. Considering the fact that Medak was contiguous to Kannada-speaking districts, significant communal violence was taking place.[3]

During the initial days of Police Action, Vazeer Ali Khan was in Hyderabad city for a week as he had to venture there every two months for his Aabkari department duties. Amena Begum and the four children were at home in Chilkepalli.

Ayoob's parents thought that their social and physical proximity to many Hindu landlords would shield them from any violence. But that was not the case. One afternoon, a crowd gathered in front of their house. It included Amena's most trusted servants. One of them, Mallesh, emerged from the horde and presented himself with folded hands. The respectful gesture was followed by a ghastly request in both Urdu and Telugu.

'*Amma, sab gaon mein gharaan dhondrein aur jalaa rein. Aap ku hum kuch nahin karte. Nemu dandam, petam meeru ekkad kelli vellandi* (Mother, everybody is searching for houses to burn in the village. We will not do anything to you. We are folding our hands in front of you; please just leave),' Mallesh appealed.

She went into the house, collected a few things and gathered her four children, among whom was the infant Ansaar, a future Indian Air Force airman who rose to become a non-commissioned officer. Once she was outside, she saw the house being burned to the ground. The roof, made of selu[4] rock, combusted before her eyes. In a matter of a few minutes, the family's fortune was up in flames. Then began her long journey to a safer haven.

From Chilkepalli to Kohir

'Do not go there. Just wait for more news,' insisted Vazeer's older sister in Hyderabad. But Vazeer did not heed her advice. At a time when Muslims faced the risk of being arrested and tortured on the mere pretext of being Razakars,[5] he set off for Chilkepalli so that he could be at the side of his wife and children. When he reached there, he stayed at the home of a Hindu friend. Amena and the children were already on the move by then. Word got around that Vazeer Ali Khan had returned. His friend's wife advised him to flee.

And so, Vazeer leapt like a tiger over the boundary of thorn plants that left splotches of blood on his body. In the dark of the night, he continued his journey to find his family. Luckily, he found them in a nearby village. It was an arduous journey back to the home of Amena's maternal family in Kohir, 15 kilometres away.

Ayoob told me about an anecdote that his parents had often repeated. One night, they had reached a rivulet that had swollen because of the rains. His parents could not risk crossing the water body with all their children at once. First, they took two children across the water. On the other side, Amena instructed the eldest, Nawab Begum, to stand still as she went over and brought the other children. Nawab Begum failed to comprehend the instructions in her drowsy state.

When Amena Begum returned, she did not find Nawab Begum at the place where she was told to remain. Amena began looking for her frantically in the pitch dark. Whenever she came upon a shadow, Amena would mistake it for her daughter and embrace it. Finally, Nawab Begum was found some distance away from where she had been left. In the morning, when Amena Begum looked at her kurta, she saw that it was speckled with blood due to the thorny trees she had mistaken for her daughter.

The family continued trudging. At a village where they stopped, they found out that a Hindu patel (village officer) had given shelter to many Muslims who fled their homes. 'He had no compulsion to help my parents. In that frenzy of violence around him, his humanity remained intact,' praised Ayoob. Unfortunately, the patel could not offer food to the refugees. Since Amena had not eaten anything, the milk in her breasts had dried out. As her baby cried out loud for milk, Amena saw a Hindu beggar eating some jawar roti (flatbread made from sorghum flour). The beggar kindly shared her food with Amena.

Finally, they reached Kohir. A journey that normally took four hours by vehicle ended up taking eight to ten days.

To Hyderabad City

When they finally returned to Hyderabad, Vazeer found that some land that had been given to him by the Nizam's administration was taken over by the new Indian government through the Housing Board. Instead, they had to make do with a one-room tenement in Old City's Hussaini Alam area. The living conditions being unmanageable there, they soon shifted to the Chataknipura Basti near Doodh Bowli. Then they went back to the area of the Sufi Saheb Dargah, which was located between Chataknipura and the Kucha Mani Khan neighbourhood in Hussaini Alam. Their third son, Ayoob, was born in that neighbourhood in 1956, the year Hyderabad state was trifurcated.

Before Ayoob resumed his family's story, he made it a point to debunk the notion that the majority of Muslims were well-off during the Nizam's era.

He clarified, 'Many still like to think the majority of Muslims were well off during the Nizam's era. But to him well-off and educated are not always synonymous, especially within the context of princely Hyderabad. A lot of the business as well as professional classes, mostly non-Muslim, had come from elsewhere. On the other hand, the educated Muslim elite would mostly join the administration.[6]

'Muslims could be found in both the Congress and Communist Party contingencies,' Ayoob said. 'While some Hindus were not against the Nizam, a large subset of the Hindu population pushed for a Hindu state as envisioned by the Hindu Mahasabha and the Arya Samaj.'

He continued, 'While Hindu Mahasabhaites adhered to their ideology, the Congress's secular strategy upstaged them. To the surprise of many anti-Nizam leaders in the country, Pandit Jawaharlal Nehru and Sardar Patel decided to treat Osman Ali Khan differently.' The deposed ruler was offered the title of rajpramukh (governor) of Hyderabad state.

'The new Indian leadership gave unquestioned rights to the Nizam over a very large number of properties in Hyderabad. All these facts could be found in a Parliament-approved document known as the Blue Book. This Congress strategy worked to stem the potentially rising anti-Muslim tide in the state,' specified Ayoob.

In the meantime, the fortunes of Vazeer's family took a surprise turn. His sister generously offered to buy him out of his property in Chilkepalli. Ayoob counted those years that followed as among the best of his father's life. That land sale to his sister brought an influx of cash with which he could spend on things that made him happy. That included two Plymouth automobiles, one for him and another for his nephew, Basheer Miyan.

Vazeer Ali Khan had a mind of his own along with a distinctive personality. Behind his Kucha Maani Khan home in Old City's Hussaini Alam locality was a colony of gowlis (cow herders, milkmen). Vazeer had great relations with them, Marwaris and Kayasthas who lived in and around the neighbourhood. Chaudhry Maisaiah and Ratnaiah were among his closest friends.

The Winds of Change

Until the second grade, Ayoob attended an Urdu-medium school right across from his house. But his father knew that an education in English would prepare Ayoob for the future. He was soon enrolled in a newly opened English-medium school called Modern Kindergarten.

In 1964, his father contested for a seat in the Municipal Corporation. He ran on an MIM ticket from the Doodh Bowli constituency. By this time, Abdul Wahid Owaisi had taken over the party and given it a new look. The party had been consolidating its presence in the Old City, a traditional stronghold. In the 1960 municipal elections, Majlis had nineteen winning candidates from the thirty it fielded. Only two Muslim candidates from the Congress won in that election.[7]

Come 1964, Vazeer lost the election.[8] Ayoob felt that his father's friends had unnecessarily prodded him into spending money to contest the seat. It was a financial blow for the family.

Meanwhile, a new population from Andhra had settled down in Hussaini Alam. Ayoob painted a picture of the cosmopolitan, secular character of the area he grew up in during the 1960s—one that bore resemblance to the Dar-us-Salaam area that my father experienced during his childhood.

'In City High School, the majority of students were Muslims. There was a Chaouche[9] of Yemeni ancestry named Ahmed Bin Sayeed Bahammam, Dharam Pal from Purana Pul and Paulson from Shah Ali Banda,' he reminisced. 'We never grew up as Hindus versus Muslims.'

With respect to the shifting social dynamics of that time, Ayoob went on to narrate an incident during which one of his close acquaintances took exception to a pejorative that I have heard many of my extended family members use. This close acquaintance was Tirpatamma, a neighbour who used to frequent Ayoob's house. Like Amena, Tirpatamma was someone who spoke her mind.

Ayoob recalled, 'One time in front of her, I said, "*Woh dher aaya tha idhar* (That dher came here)."'

Though not incensed, Tirpatamma gently objected to his use of the term dher despite the fact that it was not directed at her. '*Chunnu Sahib, dher nahin bolna. Woh gaali hai ab* (Chunnu Saahib, do not use the word dher. It is an insult now).'

Dher is a derogatory term for lower-caste Hindus that is uttered by many Muslims as well as certain upper-caste Hindus. Usually, someone's dark complexion is enough to get them labelled as a dher. Many lower-caste Telangana Hindus who performed bonded labour were referred to by this term as were those who carried out household work.

That incident alone prompted Ayoob to stop using the racist, casteist term.

Ayoob and his family were also close to Yadi Bhai and Bai Amma, Tirpatamma's children. Even in the pockets that were communally polarizing, he felt comfortable.

As the winds of change blew through in his cosmopolitan neighbourhood, Ayoob was building a solid base of the skills that would lead him to a successful career in journalism.

Books as Gateways to Another World

Ayoob's first mentor was his high-school English teacher Mr Chari, who offered him extra tuition at his house in Aghapura at 6 a.m. on some days of the week. In college, he found his second English mentor, Keshav Rao Jadhav. Jadhav had participated in the 1952 Mulki agitation, protesting against government jobs going to those from the Madras Presidency.

'I used to read Urdu books very fast. I also liked reading Urdu magazines like *Shama, Beesvi Sadi* and *Shabistan*. People used to think I was crazy because of this passion I had for reading.' Ayoob told me.

Reading the Tirath Ram Firozpuri-authored Urdu translations of well-known authors like Agatha Christie provided an early introduction to the English language and its literature. Padma Rao, who ran the SSR Library in Hussaini Alam, suggested that he read R.K. Narayan's *The English Teacher*.

This extra help enabled him to gain proficiency in English. After all, the environment that Ayoob grew up in did not provide a lot of exposure to the language. On top of that, Vazeer could not afford to send his son to a prestigious convent school. As Jadhav, Chari and Rao helped pave the road to another world for him via the English language and its literature, he pursued BiPC (biology, physics and chemistry) for intermediate studies.

Vazeer died in 1970. By that time, Ayoob's elder sister was married and two of his brothers were doing well in their jobs. With all this playing out, a career change was on the cards.

Changing Lanes

Despite being on the science track while pursuing a BSc in Zoology at City College, Ayoob realized that he was not cut out for the sciences. He had a literary temperament, but there were no family connections or acquaintances who understood the world of letters and could guide these proclivities.

While at City College, he did not attend most of his zoology classes. As for the ones he did attend, he found them incomprehensible. Much to the dismay of Amena, who was busy navigating her family through economic woes, he decided to not continue with the science route by forgoing the BSc final year exam. Fortunately, he found an arts programme at OU that was more aligned with his true calling and also took into account the two years he spent pursuing the first BSc degree.

At the end of 1974, he was offered a job as a proofreader at *Daily News*, which paid anywhere from Rs 100 to Rs 150 per month. To supplement his income, he tutored a few children.

'I started my day at dawn by juggling tuitions and my studies. Then I would ride my bicycle all the way from Hussaini Alam to the *Daily News* office in Nampally. Until I actually witnessed the printing taking place, which used to happen after 1 a.m. sometimes, I could not go back home,' Ayoob remembered. This was his routine until 1977, when he began his second undergraduate degree, a Bachelor's in Communications and Journalism (BCJ) at OU.

Ayoob was happy to be pursuing a degree that seemed to be more in line with his interests, but money proved to be an impediment. 'To pay the hefty Rs 5,000 tuition fees, my brothers Mir Abul Mani Khan and Mir Ansaar Ali Khan came to my rescue.'

He met his future wife Nasreen during the BCJ days. Right after completing the degree, he could have taken a job in the public relations department at the Electronics Corporation of India. Taking up that role would have undoubtedly eased his financial situation. Instead, with financial help and encouragement from Nasreen, he did a Master's in Communication and Journalism (MCJ).

'Upon finishing my MCJ at twenty-three, my mental makeup took shape and I had the tools to become a proper journalist. After completing an internship with UNI, the bureau chief, D. Sitaram, hired me as a cub reporter in 1979,' Ayoob elaborated.

He got married to Nasreen around this time. Her London-based brother happened to be in town then. She told him, 'If you are serious about getting married, now is the time because my brother is here; he can convince everyone in my family.'

The union went as planned but when their first child was born on 24 December 1980, life came at him hard and fast. Ayoob admitted that his financial situation made it hard to handle things at the time. That is when he set off for a place where many Hyderabadis were seeking their fortune.

1970s' Saudi Arabia: A Major Outpost for Hyderabadis

Arshad Pirzada, Ayoob's childhood friend from the City High School, had already moved to Saudi Arabia in 1976. In four years, he had built a respectable life for himself, working his way up from store assistant to counter salesman at an automotive component store in Riyadh. His progress was in tandem with the Kingdom's, which was benefitting greatly from the oil boom. The 1970s was the decade when oil money began to trickle down. The consumer economy had just begun to boom with the Hondas and Nissans coming into the country at an unprecedented rate.

Ayoob followed these developments from afar, hearing about it from the families of many Hyderabadis who had made the move. He told Arshad he wanted to try his luck in Saudi. But cobbling together the money to purchase an Azad visa was a problem—the going rate in those days was Rs 50,000 to Rs 100,000.

In 1978, Arshad sponsored his brother Nadeem's Azad visa. He promised Ayoob that he would bring him over next. True to his word, he sponsored Ayoob's visa in a few months. His employer on paper was a company named Lilbulook, but like many aspiring expatriates, he used this permit to find a job that was more aligned to his interest and qualifications.

Arriving in the Kingdom

Ayoob landed in Saudi Arabia on 16 October 1981. Back then, the Riyadh airport was no more than a shed and a couple of runways, and he remembered walking to the small terminal building from the tarmac. From the window of his taxi, he saw a skyline dominated by massive cranes. The entire city seemed like it was under construction—mud buildings were transforming into modern, concrete structures.

At Arshad's modest lodgings, he met Nasrullah Omar Khalidi, who used to work as a librarian at King Saud University. Khalidi was a reservoir of knowledge on Hyderabad's history. Sitting cross-legged on a rug in Arshad's living room and sipping tea, the three men would often talk late into the night about the neighbourhoods and the people of their home city.

Unlike many Hyderabadis who had moved to Saudi, Ayoob did not want to apply for vocational jobs like those of an electrician or engineer. He wanted to work in journalism. At the time, there were only two English newspapers in Saudi—*Arab News* and *Saudi Gazette*.

Khalidi tapped into his vast network of media professionals and academics for his journalist friend. One of Khalidi's father's acquaintances headed the Islamic Economics department at King Abdul Aziz University. Ayoob went to meet an Aligarh-educated economist named Mohammed Najaatullah Siddiqui. Siddiqui instructed Ayoob to see a senior journalist named Tariq Ghazi at *Saudi Gazette*. He gave the young journalist a card on which he wrote, 'The bearer of this card is known to me. Please help.'

Ayoob recollected, 'When I took that card to Ghazi at the *Gazette*'s Jeddah headquarters, Ghazi put in a good word for me to his editor, Saud Al-Islam, who then asked that I be interviewed. I was then hired.'

One order of business remained—he had to transfer the ownership of his visa from his 'sponsor' to his new employer, *Saudi Gazette*. It would be a few months before that happened. While he was waiting for that formality to be fulfilled, Ayoob spent the downtime at Arshad's house reading, watching movies or passing time at Arshad's brother's travel agency.

Expatriate Life

Living arrangements in Jeddah bordered on dormitory-style. In his first accommodation, Ayoob was the eighth tenant in a three-room flat. The men were on a weekly roster to cook and clean for all the others. Ayoob, the pampered Hyderabadi, had never washed his own clothes before. Sitting on the mattress in one of his early accommodations, he had a moment of truth.

'I thought to myself, "Where the hell am I?" This was more down-at-heels than an obscure locality in Hyderabad's Old City,' Ayoob laughed as he recalled those early days of struggle in Saudi.

My father had told me something similar about his early days in the Gulf. But it was also their making. Many upper-class Hyderabadi Muslims had lived through these humbling experiences while starting out in the Kingdom. '*Hum logon ki akhal thikaane aayi* (Our heads were finally screwed back on straight),' Ayoob told me.

One thing that these men (and it was mostly men—the families would join them later) did have was each other. An unspoken honour code also developed between the Hyderabadis coming to try their luck in the Kingdom and the more established ones who housed them. There was an implicit understanding that when they had become more financially stable, they would pay back the friend who had hosted them when they were newcomers. There was also the idea that they would pay it back by hosting a new migrant when their financial situation improved.

Ayoob told me that there was no subverting the ingrained hierarchies of Saudi Arabia. South Asians often found themselves on the bottom of that chain. He mentioned the rudeness with which law enforcement officials spoke to South Asian expatriates. In the event that a South Asian had the misfortune to be involved in a road accident with an Arab, the first thing he would usually be asked by the police was the following question: 'How could you afford such a vehicle?'

'They saw themselves as masters and us as "rafeeqs" in "their" country,' stated Ayoob. *Rafeeq* is an Arabic word whose literal meaning is 'friend', but it has another implied meaning—'slave'. Despite these hierarchies, Ayoob had a fruitful tenure with *Saudi Gazette*. It was an interesting time to be working for the outlet, which played a key role in chronicling the transformation of Saudi's economic fortunes. It was also an exciting place to work: there were reporters from the UK, America, Pakistan and The Philippines. The oil money meant that the city was constantly in a state of construction. Ayoob recounted that sometimes the sound of jackhammers drilling through concrete would wake him up in the early hours of the morning.

Thrown into the Deep End

In 1983, an American senior level reporter who specialized in financial journalism suddenly resigned. Khan was asked to step into his shoes. 'I had never done any business reporting,' he told me. 'I dabbled in everything by doing general stories. Suddenly, I had to reorient myself and show my colleagues that I belonged in this position.'

A year on, Khan was promoted to chief reporter. 'That is when I began reading up more on Islamic history and the tribal societies of the Gulf,' Khan noted, 'Had I not done that, I would not have left a mark at the *Gazette*.' His new and hard-earned knowledge opened many doors. He also developed a sharper understanding of the dynamics between the various Arab states. Officials he interviewed were more forthcoming with him because he deeply understood the context of Saudi society. The Kingdom's sheikhs were wary of the media, especially the international outlets that had portrayed them as backward hedonists who gambled in Paris over a weekend and enjoyed the company of women a bit too much.

Soon, Khan was appointed as the deputy managing editor, in charge of not just Saudi Arabia but international affairs as well. One correspondent who worked under him for a little while went on to become a famous journalist and a dissident of the Kingdom—Jamal Khashoggi. After Khashoggi was killed at the Saudi consulate in Istanbul, several profiles described him as someone who harboured Islamist tendencies but then went on to become an insider of the royal family. Ayoob told me that when they worked together, Khashoggi came across as someone who had a mind of his own.

But it was his interview with Zia-ul-Haq, then Pakistani President, that Ayoob described as the high point of his career. When Ayoob and his Pakistani colleague Mazhar asked Zia how close Pakistan was to finishing a nuclear bomb, he had used both his hands to suggest they were a couple of screws away from completion. When the shocked reporters asked Zia if they could quote him as he made this revelation, he told them to keep the device with which they recorded the interview on.

The moment Ayoob told his editor about the sensational comment that had the Indian and Pakistani consulates frantically calling the *Gazette*, his superior took away the tape so that he could plausibly deny possession of it. That evening, Zia's quote was plastered on the front page of the *Saudi Gazette* as a banner headline.

Another compelling encounter Ayoob had was with a namesake— Dr Ayyub Thakur, a nuclear physicist from the Kashmir Valley who was in exile and teaching at King Abdul Aziz University. When Ayoob was covering the Hajj season, Thakur had invited him to his tent in the Arafat plain outside of Mecca. 'We need your help. You are a Muslim. That is why you should help us with the cause by giving us coverage,' Thakur implored.

When Ayoob kindly refused, Thakur told him, 'You do not have an understanding of the subcontinent. Your reading of history is limited.'

The Expatriate Life Comes to an End

In the middle of 1998, Ayoob had to make an important decision. The choices in front of him were to stay for a few more years in Saudi Arabia or head back to Hyderabad. If he remained in the Kingdom, he could probably have become one of the foremost commentators on the Middle East. But if he did not return to Hyderabad then, there was a chance he would not be employable.

'Had I stayed in Saudi Arabia, the chances of an Indian media outlet hiring a veteran with more than forty years on the job would be very slim,' he affirmed.

It was a turning point for his children too. His elder son Muneeb had finished seventh grade at the Indian Embassy School and his second son Mujeeb was in the fourth grade. Now was the time to pull them out of Saudi Arabia and transfer them to schools in India—this would give them enough time to prepare for the all-important board examinations. He wanted them to move out of Saudi Arabia because unlike Western countries, the Kingdom did not provide a path to naturalization; at some point, he felt, they would have to return to India.

The ducks had lined up. It was time for Ayoob to go back home.

Back to Hyderabad

Soon after he returned, one of his friends told him that *Deccan Chronicle* was looking for someone to write about Hyderabad on a freelance basis. He caught the eye of its chief editor, A.T. Jayanti, after filing a few stories on the cultural and historical aspects of Hyderabad, including some events that were taking place at the Qutub Shahi tombs.

When they met face-to-face, she suggested he meet T. Venkatram Reddy, the owner of the newspaper. 'Do meet Mr Reddy. But let me say this. I do not know anything about the countries you have visited and the issues you learned about. Unfortunately, such coverage is not required by us,' advised Jayanti. Reddy emphasized the same thing about their need for more local, not international news.

But Ayoob was up to the task. He asserted, 'I am from here and I know the city. Tell me what has to be written and then I will decide.'

Ayoob brought a distinct flavour to the newsroom. Even though Jayanti was a Bombay-bred Tamilian who was not as acquainted with Hyderabad, she valued Ayoob's insights into the city and state's princely history. Narayan Keshavan, a bright trainee journalist with *The Hindu* at the time, told Ayoob that he had been asked to not seek out 'those Muslim stories'.

The Times of India and the Telangana Turmoil

As he continued bringing Hyderabad's rich past to the fore, Ayoob eventually became *Deccan Chronicle's* bureau chief. In 2006, he made the move to *The Times of India*, where he became the special affairs editor. Regardless of which stories could be considered 'Muslim' or not, Ayoob maintained that the city was and is still home to a Muslim minority that comprises 40 per cent of the population, a lot of whom had been taking to English. Author and former TOI resident editor Kingshuk Nag helped Ayoob capture this upwardly mobile market that had been gradually acquiring purchasing power in the last few decades.

Ayoob recalled a meeting where Nag had tasked him to present his ideas for increasing readership. Business executives from TOI's Mumbai head office had also come to Hyderabad to assess the city's market potential. The conversation turned to Telangana versus Andhra. 'You Telangana people did not have anything before we arrived. We built this city,' commented a marketing head who was from Andhra.

Ayoob could not let that barb slide.

'You came and destroyed Hyderabad's culture. It was a cosmopolitan culture despite certain flaws,' he responded.

The marketing manager shot back, 'We gave you a film industry.'

'You gave us obscenity. There was no obscenity in Telugu films. Look at it now,' replied Ayoob.

This anecdote illustrates that Ayoob felt passionately about the issue of Telangana's statehood. As an editor, he helped amplify voices that called for a separate state. One such person included Diwakar Reddy, a former minister from the Rayalaseema region of united Andhra Pradesh. Reddy claimed that the Coastal Andhra culture was different from that of Rayalaseema's. His proposal was for a state that combined Rayalaseema and Telangana.[10] Indeed, parts of Rayalaseema were once under the Nizam's dominions; over time, the Nizams had ceded Kurnool, Anantapur, Kadapa, Chittoor and Bellary (now in Karnataka) to the British.

'By no means did I advocate for racial, religious or ethnolinguistic superiority,' Ayoob clarified, 'just equality. Because we did not have that here, I endorsed the idea of a separate state.'

A Splintering Hyderabad

As our conversation neared its end, Ayoob unequivocally asserted that Police Action did not affect the brotherly relations among Hindus and Muslims of Hyderabad when it came to daily interactions. 'Everybody eventually recovered from that trauma,' he mentioned.

Something flipped in the 1970s. During the Ganesh festival that year, the Bharatiya Jan Sangh, predecessor to the BJP, put up banners proclaiming that India be declared a Hindu republic. In retaliation, a Muslim man hurled a rock at a saffron-daubed stone that marked a site of worship at the foot of the Charminar. Later, a Muslim driver rammed a public transport bus into the stone. The site would grow into a temple.[11]

The Hindus retaliated to the attack on the stone by desecrating a mosque located in the compound of a Muslim-owned factory. Then Chief Minister N.T. Rama Rao did step in and promised to repair the mosque. But the seeds of communal discord had been sown. The fault lines became even more visible after Ramiza Bi's rape. Ramiza Bi was the wife of a rickshaw-puller who had been murdered by the police. When she went to file a complaint at a police station, she was sexually assaulted by the law enforcement officials. The riots that took place in the wake of this ghastly incident further splintered the city.[12]

Ayoob spoke about another incident from 1984.[13] 'When a few Muslims in a Mangal Haat mosque were killed, NTR entered the mosque, sat there on dharna (a peaceful demonstration) and demanded the arrest of those who perpetrated the killings,' he remembered.

As the former DC bureau chief and TOI special affairs editor steered our conversation to more contemporary times, his assessment of the communal atmosphere was rather pragmatic. 'Today, there is an undercurrent of hatred, but it has not seeped into the common citizens of Hyderabad. However, the communal agenda of the BJP is gaining strength. By raking up the past excesses of the Razakars, they are trying to whip up mob frenzies,' Ayoob remarked.

The movie *Razakar: A Silent Genocide of Hyderabad* sought to do just that. Madhavi Latha, of Virinchi Hospital fame, implored people to watch the propaganda film during her Lok Sabha campaign.[14]

The movie showcases the kind of revisionist distortion of Hyderabad's history that Ayoob has been constantly fighting against. Now, there is a younger generation of journalists keeping the flag flying. Talented reporters like Serish Nanisetti, Yunus Lasania and Syed Mohammed are continuing the work that Ayoob pioneered in the English media landscape of Hyderabad.

Ali Adil Khan: The Double Migration

مجھے بھی لمحۂ ہجرت نے کر دیا تقسیم

نگاہ گھر کی طرف ہے قدم سفر کی طرف

— شہپر رسول

Mujhe bhi lamha-e-hijrat ne kar diya taqseem
Nigah ghar ki taraf hai qadam safar ki taraf

My existence too was partitioned the moment
I uprooted myself
As I keep trudging onward, my glance still veers
towards home

—Shehpar Rasool

Hyderabad and Karachi in Canada

Brampton, a town about forty minutes outside of Toronto, has a Sikh population so large that one can jokingly refer to it as the sixth centre of Sikhism. The long walk from the Bramalea GO station to Baig's Grill, through what looks a lot like typical North American suburbia, is punctuated by trucking companies and Punjabi eateries. On picket

94

signs outside small buildings, there are photographs of attorneys with the names Singh and Kaur. Upon arriving at Kennedy Road, one can see Village of India, the Punjabi restaurant that was known to be a haunt of the late singer Sidhu Moosewala.

Baig's Grill is right next to Village of India. When chef and owner Ahmed Baig opened this restaurant, he had two goals in mind: bringing Hyderabad's distinct mix of Mughlai and south Indian flavours to the Greater Toronto Area; and recreating the menu of the Orient Hotel, an iconic dining establishment from Hyderabad's yesteryears.

I was at Baig's Grill that fall afternoon to meet with Ali Adil Khan, an Indo-Pakistani Canadian with roots in Hyderabad. Our Mississauga-based mutual acquaintance had told me that Khan's maternal grandfather, Nawab Liaquat Jung Bahadur, had served as finance minister in princely Hyderabad.

Adil, in his early sixties now, is a senior executive at LTIMindtree, a subsidiary of India's construction giant Larsen & Toubro. He is also a well-known patron of the arts in Toronto's South Asian community. Adil made a movie star entry to our meeting. He pulled up in a black Porsche Macan, stepping out dressed in a dapper suit and sunglasses. As Ahmed served us some biryani and lukhmis—square-shaped samosas stuffed with minced meat—Adil and I chatted about his life. The story of his family is one that spanned three different countries.

Osmanshahi: A Neighbourhood on the Banks of the Moosi

Back in Hyderabad, the echo of the kirtans from the gurdwara blends into the cacophony of the sanitary shops lining Afzalgunj Road which is just outside of Old City. There are rows of apartment complexes above the hardware and textiles stores that lead to the banks of the Moosi River, which separates the 'Old' and 'New' parts of the city. On 20 October 1930, Adil's father Mohammad Anwaruddin Ali was born in this part of Hyderabad.

Not too long after that, the Ali family moved to the Aghapura area near my father's native Dar-us-Salaam locality. They then temporarily shifted to the Red Hills area, while Anwar's father, Mohammad Ishaq Ali, was getting a six-bedroom house constructed in New Aghapura.

As the head of Central Stores in the Nizam's postal services, Ishaq handled the storage and distribution of the stationary, furniture, fixtures and stamps for the city's postal department. When his son Anwar started the tenth grade, he was transferred to Gulbarga as the division head. Upon finishing his matric from Nutan Vidyalaya High School there, Anwar was admitted to Nizam College in Hyderabad city. He spent some of his summers at his uncle's Nizamabad estate, where rice, lentils, vegetables and exotic fruits were cultivated.

Bidar Bombarded

In the fateful year of 1948, Ishaq Ali ended up being transferred to Bidar. During Operation Polo, Ishaq happened to be in Hyderabad city for work. Anwar, who was seventeen then, was in Bidar when the Indian troops marched in. When Anwar heard fighter planes roaring and bombs going off, he and his family left the city and moved towards the villages. The Indian Army was mostly sticking to the urban areas as it marched towards Hyderabad city. Still, there would be at least 500 deaths reported from Bidar district as a result of Operation Polo. When Anwar returned to Bidar city after the storm had passed, he found that their house had been ransacked and looted.

Adil told me that his father was no sympathizer of Qasim Razvi, who he felt had carelessly led young people to the battlefield to get massacred. 'The general impression was that the Razakar chief was ill-prepared to take on the Indian Army. He more or less sent them to the battlefield with sticks,' he acknowledged. In his memoir titled *The Tragedy of Hyderabad*, Mir Laiq Ali, the last Prime Minister of Hyderabad, who also happened to be Ishaq Ali's second cousin,

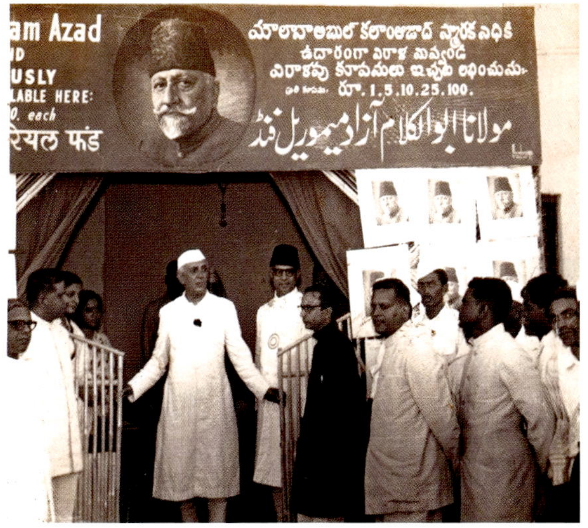

Nehru and Abid Ali Khan at Maulana Azad Memorial Fund; second from Jawaharlal Nehru's right is Khan

Courtesy of Siasat Archives

Author's grandfather, M.A. Ghaffar

Author's collection

A gathering put together by the *Payaam* newspaper; Abid Ali Khan is in the bottom row, third from the left

Courtesy of Siasat Archives

Umar Faruq Quadri (in the keffiyeh scarf) leading anti-CAA-NRC protests at MANUU

Courtesy of Umar Faruq Quadri

A.Q. Sarwari meeting Rajendra Prasad

Courtesy of Vasiq Sarwari

Bakshi Ghulam Mohammad inaugurating the Idara-e-Adabiyat-e-Urdu

Courtesy of Idara-e-Adabiyat-e-Urdu

Dr Zor with Syed Sajjad Zaheer and others; Zaheer, one of the founders of the Progressive Writers' Association, is third from the left in the front row

Courtesy of Idara-e-Adabiyat-e-Urdu

Dr Zor with some renowned Urdu poets. Sitting on the takht from left to right: Jigar Moradabadi, Amjad Hyderabadi and Josh Malihabadi.

Courtesy of Vasiq Sarwari

Nehru inaugurating the Urdu Hall in 1955. A few people in this picture are: Habib-ur-Rahman, Fazl-ur-Rahman, Padmaja Naidu, Abid Ali Khan, Syeed Jung, Burgula Ramakrishna Rao, Ghulam Yazdani, Mandumula Narsing Rao and others.

Courtesy of Siasat Archives

Sarojni Naidu visits Idara. On her right is Mohiuddin Qadri Zor. The person with the glasses on the left in the second row is A.Q. Sarwari.

Courtesy of Siasat Archives

The Idara University that Dr Zor envisioned

Source: Idara-e-Adabiyat-e-Urdu

The Idara-e-Adabiyat-e-Urdu building today

Photo credit: Abdullahi Abdulrahman

Mir Ayoob Ali Khan with Zia-ul-Haq

Courtesy of Mir Ayoob Ali Khan

Mir Ayoob Ali Khan's mother, Amena Begum, in 1983

Courtesy of Mir Ayoob Ali Khan

Mir Ayoob Ali Khan shaking hands with Prince Abdullah bin Abdulaziz

Courtesy of Mir Ayoob Ali Khan

Ali Adil Khan with Ishaq Ali at his Bismillah in Hyderabad, Sindh. The Bismillah ceremony, which marks the beginning of a child commencing the Qur'an, at one time was a huge occasion in Hyderabadi Muslim households. Even in 1960s' Pakistan, Adil's family ensured that it was celebrated as such.

Courtesy of Ali Adil Khan

Ali Adil Khan with his family. From left to right: Adnan Ali Khan (son), Shehla Khan (wife), Haniya Khan (daughter-in-law) holding Ayaan Ali Khan (grandson), Ali Adil Khan and Nadia Mahnoor Khan (daughter).

Courtesy of Ali Adil Khan

Young Sampathamma Rao

Courtesy of Apparasu Srinivasa Rao

Young Apparasu Sheshagiri Rao

Courtesy of Apparasu Srinivasa Rao

Anwar Ali and Ishaq Ali

Courtesy of Ali Adil Khan

The banned Jayprakash Narayan rally in 1947
Courtesy of Siasat Archives

Raj Bahadur Gour with Nusrat Mohiuddin and K.L. Mahendra. From left to right: Nusrat Mohiuddin (Makhdoom Mohiuddin's son), K.L. Mahendra and Raj Bahadur Gour.

Courtesy of Oudesh Rani Bawa

OU Comrades' Association. From left to right: Jawad Razvi, Raj Bahadur Gour, Manik Lal Gupta, Alam Khundmiri, Omkar Pershad, Syed Ibrahim and Qutub-e-Alam.

Courtesy of Oudesh Rani Bawa

Oudesh Rani Bawa with Raj Bahadur Gour
Courtesy of Oudesh Rani Bawa

Rai Mehboob Narayan and Rai Mehboob Rai
Courtesy of Oudesh Rani Bawa

Narayan Raj Saxena's great-grandfather,
Bansi Raja

Raj with comrades. Standing left to right: Burgula
Narsing Rao and Jawad Razvi. Seated left to right:
Omkar Pershad and Raj Bahadur Gour.

Muhammad Ali Jinnah's visit to Hyderabad; the first person on Jinnah's left is MIM chief,
Bahadur Yar Jung

Nizam Mir Osman Ali Khan at Malwala Palace, a major bastion of the Mathur biradari
Courtesy of Siasat Archives

Nizam Mir Osman Ali Khan laying the foundation stone of a church
Courtesy of Siasat Archives

attested to how the Majlis Ittehad-ul-Muslimeen had bitten off more than it could chew. During a rally organized by the MIM for the Nizam's birthday in May 1947, Razvi was scouring the crowd of 50,000 people to see if they possessed any arms that could be collected by the Razakars.[1] It was a doomed project right from the start. The Majlis militia would be no match for the five army columns and air force of the Indian Army.

Back in Bidar, Anwar was part of a group of young Muslim men who were rounded up and questioned by the Army. He was let go once the questioners were convinced that he had no ties to the Razakars. Still, the family felt that it would not be safe to stick around in Bidar. Hyderabad had not seen as much carnage as some of the other areas. Besides, Ishaq Ali was there. A local Hindu friend of Ishaq's arranged for their safe passage to the train station and had someone accompany them to Hyderabad.

There may not have been as much violence in Hyderabad, but there was a sense among the city's Muslims that something had changed forever. Those who worked for the Nizam's administration, like Ishaq Ali, suddenly found themselves out of favour and luck. It was clear as day that the old order had passed, and the new military dispensation of the Indian government had different ideas about what they wanted the city to be. In these circumstances, many Muslims had begun to consider migrating to Pakistan.

Pakistan Calling

As life limped back to normalcy, Anwar rejoined the first year of his BSc programme at OU. In spite of struggling initially, he obtained his degree with distinction. Soon after, Anwar had a long discussion with his father on their future, something that a lot of Hyderabadi Muslims were contemplating. Given that Adil's father was the oldest of five siblings, Adil said that there was pressure on him to earn money or at least get another degree that would lead to a high-paying job.

Two choices lay in front of him—either pursue further studies at the Aligarh Muslim University or migrate to Pakistan for better economic prospects.

In the Sindh province where education levels were very low, migrants from India got important positions in the banking system. Notably, a number of Hyderabadis who had crossed over secured jobs in the State Bank of Pakistan.[2] Anwar's uncle, Arif, was already in Karachi, where many doctors who had studied at OU were settling down.

'There is no better time to move to Karachi, with opportunities in abundance there for young graduates,' Arif advised his nephew during a visit to Hyderabad in 1949.

After Ishaq Ali's relative, who was also an assistant in the postal department, arranged a migration permit, Anwar boarded a ship from Bombay to Karachi. He reached Pakistan on 14 August 1950, the day on which the country turned three. For the first few days, he stayed in a rest house in the Manghopir area; after that, he went to his uncle's house in Pir Ilahi Baksh Colony.

In less than a week, he sought admission at an engineering college in Lahore. Unfortunately, the new student intake was closed until next year. When he returned to Karachi, there was an offer to become an instructor at the Pakistan Air Force Training College. He gave the final tests at the Air Force Headquarters in Rawalpindi. But that opportunity did not pan out.

On the advice of his grandfather, Anwar also reached out to his father's second cousin, Mir Laiq Ali. The last Prime Minister of Hyderabad also migrated to Pakistan, but under rather different circumstances—he had escaped house arrest by the Indian Government after sneaking out in a burqa and then catching a flight from Bombay to Karachi.[3] In what was the first capital of Pakistan, Laiq Ali became a founder and major trustee of an entity that resettled Hyderabadi immigrants and helped young men land job opportunities.

The Hyderabad Trust

The last Prime Minister of princely Hyderabad was already an influential figure in the early days of Pakistan. The new country drafted him to serve as their special emissary to the US to request a $2 billion loan for immediate economic, agricultural, industrial, service and defence expenditures.[4] He then served as an advisor in Pakistan's defence ministry.[5]

Laiq Ali had established the Hyderabad Trust (HT) with the Rs 2 million kitty that the seventh Nizam had gifted Pakistan before Police Action.[6] The Trust was active in allotting houses, granting land, disbursing stipends and facilitating pensions for Hyderabadi migrants.[7] The Liaquat National Hospital was also set up under its aegis.[8]

One day, Anwar received a personal call from Laiq Ali. He had called to tell Anwar that he had been selected for industrial training in Ohio.

A New World

Anwar arrived in New York City on 1 May 1951. Adil recalled the awe on his father's face when he talked about viewing the New York skyline from his PIA flight. In a few days, the twenty-one-year-old Anwar reached Cleveland, where he would begin training at the Columbia Match Factory. Mrs Smith, the elderly secretary to the factory manager Carl Weaver, offered him a room at $6 per week.

The factory was nothing like the feudal setup of princely Hyderabad, where families like Anwar's had live-in servants who cooked, cleaned and cleared after their masters. In the factory, the work culture was such that Anwar had to contribute to physical tasks like lifting heavy tools and equipment. He recalled being shocked at seeing the factory's president himself cleaning up some trash with a broom and throwing it in the bin.

The professionally enriching and eye-opening five months in the US came to an end in 1951. Before heading back to Karachi, he had stopovers in Paris, Dusseldorf, Berlin and Brussels, where he visited glass, textile, dynamite and chemical manufacturing facilities. Upon returning to Pakistan, he was appointed as a high-ranking officer at a new match factory inaugurated by Governor General Ghulam Muhammad.

The Nuptials

In the 1950s, travel between India and Pakistan was more or less frictionless. When Anwar heard about the passing of his grandfather, he flew from Karachi to Bombay. From there, he took a train to Hyderabad's Nampally station where he was received by one of his uncles.

The family could not have been prouder of their Pakistani relative, who was impeccably dressed in an American suit. A few days after he landed, Anwar's mother told him she wanted to see him married. She had already done the groundwork, by narrowing the search for a bride to three girls from respectable families. One of the girls, Bilquis Nazneen, belonged to their old Osmanshahi neighbourhood. Her father Nawab Liaquat Jung Bahadur and future father-in-law Ishaq Ali had also been childhood friends and schoolmates. Within fifteen days, Anwar and his family arrived to the bride's palatial residence called Laal Bangla, where the union was solemnized. The newlyweds then travelled to Agra and Delhi for their honeymoon.

Back in Karachi, they began living in a rented house in the Malir area. As someone who had servants at her beck and call in Hyderabad, it was difficult for Bilquis to adjust to life in a rental home. 'Having to fetch her own water and living in a house with just one bathroom did not come easy to her,' Adil revealed.

Until 1956, Anwar worked in the private match factory of Khairpur, Sindh, as its head of marketing. He would travel the length and breadth of East and West Pakistan to promote its product. Soon, the 1965 War put the first spokes in the wheel of travel between India and Pakistan. Anwar and Bilquis made several trips back to Hyderabad before those restrictions were put in place. Adil was born in Hyderabad in 1961, on one of those trips.

Soon, the Khairpur match factory was taken over by the Wazir Ali Industries Group. When a shortage of wood halted operations in Khairpur, Anwar was transferred to a town that had the same name as his birthplace.

In Sindh's Hyderabad, he worked as a manager in a cotton factory. Due to his training in the US and previous manufacturing experience, he did well in his role of supervising construction and the installation of machinery. Anwar's aptitude and honesty ensured that he kept getting promotions.

Adil's brother, Asim, too, was born in Hyderabad—the one in Sindh.

'"Hyderabadi" Mohajir Pakistani' or Just 'Hyderabadi Pakistani'?

In Karachi, many people from the Deccan ended up settling down in enclaves like Bahadurabad and Pir Ilahi Baksh Colony. There were some social associations, but they were often confined to people from specific educational institutions like Hyderabad city's Mahbubia Girls School or Osmania University.[9]

Talking about his early years in Karachi, Adil reminisced, 'Growing up in Pakistan in the 1960s was good. We were still being raised as Hyderabadis. When coming back from school, we were expected to change into white kurta pajamas.'

As children, Adil and his brother learnt Urdu from their maternal grandmother, who had also moved to Karachi, which is why they picked up some quirks of the Deccan accent. Khan gave me the example of the Urdu letter 'qaaf (ق)'. In the north Indian-influenced Urdu, its guttural sound is voiced by pressing the root of the tongue on the throat. In the Deccan accent, the sound comes across as 'khe'—less guttural and flatter. Repeating one of his grandmother's lessons on how to say the following sentence, Adil recited, '*Khaaid-e-Azam ki mazaar pe khawa baithaawa hai aur "khaain khaain" kar raai* (Sitting atop the mausoleum of Quaid-e-Azam, the crow cries "caw caw")'.

Adil also picked up some Dakhani vocabulary. He replied with 'hao' instead of the orthodox 'haan' or even the 'nakko' in lieu of 'nahin'. Some of these quirks of people from the Deccan were already being made fun of in Pakistani pop culture. In the late 1970s, the comedian Majid Jahangir caricatured the Hyderabadi accent on a sketch comedy show.[10]

This ridicule was common even as some of the country's most famous writers and public personalities had their origins in Hyderabad state. Anwar Maqsood was a star presenter on Pakistan's national television channel PTV. His sister Fatima Suraiya[11] went on to become a renowned drama writer.

The Ali family was not unaffected by the lampoonery and caricaturing. Khan told me that they sometimes wondered whether they had made the right decision by coming to Pakistan. In the national imagination, the Hyderabadis were considered a part of the group known as Mohajirs, literally meaning migrant in Urdu. These were the non-Punjabi migrants who had come over to Pakistan, mostly from north, central and south India.

During the first eleven years of Pakistan's existence, the Mohajirs had a reasonable share in the civil administration and the military. In 1951, for instance, Mohajirs held thirty-three out of ninety-five senior positions in the Civil Service.[12] As of 1959, eleven of the forty-eight top-level military positions were held by Mohajirs.[13]

But Ayub Khan's military government changed all that. Mohajirs, who were often second-in-command behind Punjabis, were supplanted by the Pashtuns in both the bureaucracy and the military.[14]

What's in a Name?

After the 'Mulki versus non-Mulki' debate played out in the Telangana region of Andhra Pradesh, Pakistan was witnessing its own 'son-of-the-soil' movement in the 1960s. People who were born in the regions that had become Pakistan started getting preference in institutions like the armed forces.

While some Mohajirs such as Brigadier Mirza Masood Ali 'Hesky' Baig[15] from Hyderabad did achieve high ranks in the military, it was against the odds. A name with a Punjabi or Pashtun ring to it helped the chances of advancement in the military.

In the 1970s, Adil's parents had his official name changed to Ali Adil Khan from Mohammad Adil Ali. Even though his name now sounded more Pashtun, it still contained the Deccan's heritage in that the fifth sultan of Bijapur, Ali Adil Shah, had also adopted the title of Khan.

More Interesting Times in Pakistan

The seeds of the religious and cultural makeover that would take place during the regimes of Zulfiqar Ali Bhutto and General Zia-ul-Haq had been sowed during the time of Ayub Khan. There was one group of Pakistanis that felt even more short-changed than the Mohajirs—the Bengalis in the east. Their resentment bubbled over into a Liberation War that would create the nation of Bangladesh. 'My father really admired Sheikh Mujib as a leader. Bengalis really did not deserve the treatment meted out to them,' said Adil.

As President and then Prime Minister of Pakistan from 1971 to 1977, Bhutto encouraged a kind of aggressive cultural nationalism that was intense for migrants from India.

In 1973, he christened the salwar kameez as 'awaami libaas' or national dress.[16] It was a clear attempt to distance the state from the kurta-pajama, which was the standard dress of north Indian migrants from cities like Lucknow, Delhi and Allahabad. The sari, which was worn by the older women in Adil's family, began to be seen as hostile.

There was also an economic overhaul alongside the cultural one. Many industries, including cotton ginning and edible oil manufacturing, were nationalized. In 1973, Anwar Ali took on the role of commercial director of the Pakistan Edible Oil Corporation.

There was a lot of corruption and misuse of authority during this period. Ministers were brazenly profiteering from industries to bankroll election campaigns and fill their personal coffers.

After General Zia-ul-Haq ousted Bhutto and eventually had him hanged in 1979, Zia began reversing the nationalization drive of his predecessor. Though on the shop floor and at the local level, the culture of bribing and underhand activity still prevailed. It annoyed Anwar Ali, a man who stayed true to his principles. 'Sadly, with the rot that had set into various industries, my father's honesty and work ethic prevented him from rising higher. Staying away from ministers and low-level politicians alike enabled him to avoid unethical practices,' explained Khan.

Karachi on the Boil

Since the late 1970s, Mohajir students at the University of Karachi had begun organizing themselves. The All-Pakistan Mohajir Students Organisation (APMSO) was the student wing and predecessor of the political party, the Mohajir Qaumi Movement (MQM). The MQM would seek to address the sidelining of the 'Urdu-speaking' ethnicity that migrated to Pakistan at the time of Partition.

The APMSO had also established a presence at the NED University of Engineering and Technology, where Adil went to study mechanical engineering. But Adil was not a part of the MQM movement. Instead, he chose to be associated with the People's Students Federation, the student wing of the Pakistan People's Party (PPP).

After he earned his engineering degree in 1984, Adil secured a lucrative job with the oil company Schlumberger. For the next three years, he worked on oil rigs in Indonesia and Australia. Then, Adil went on to pursue an MBA at the University of Texas. He returned to Karachi after that, landing a job with the oil and gas company Exxon. At the time, Karachi had become an increasingly difficult place to live. The days were marked by violent street skirmishes between political factions like the MQM and the PPP.

The Jamaat-e-Islami Pakistan's student wing, Islami Jamiat Tulaba (IJT) and other progressive groups were also a part of these bloody turf wars.[17] It was believed that the IJT had procured its weapons from militants who had received training near the Afghanistan–Pakistan border for the Soviet-Afghan War.[18] Soon enough, arms were proliferating all around Karachi, especially on college campuses.

On the home front, Adil was being asked to get married by his mother and his aunt. '*Koi Hyderabadi potti khandan mein iss ke liye dekhne ka hai* (We have to find a Hyderabadi girl in the family for him)', they said. But Adil already had someone in mind—a classmate from NED whose office was in the same building as his.

Adil got along well with Shehla, who belonged to a family from Bhopal. She was a civil engineer who was a part of the team designing the new Karachi Airport. They got married in December of 1988.

A Second 'Hijrat'

General Zia died in 1988, leaving behind a country where Islamization was rampant. Meanwhile, the situation in Karachi had deteriorated further. The law-and-order landscape was abysmal—the papers were full of reports of violence in several parts of the city. The police machinery had broken down. It was a 'virtual civil war', in the words of one scholar, 'between the security forces of the PPP government and a heavily-armed, ethnically-based political party, the Muhajir Qaumi Mahaz (MQM or Muhajir National Front)'.[19]

The kidnapping of a neighbour's son brought this chaos into Adil's neck of the woods. Not long after, Adil's car and dog—a Yorkshire terrier named Sunny—were stolen. Matters came to a head when there was a burglary in his house. He felt it was time to leave.

His bosses at Exxon urged him to stay back, citing a bright future for him at the firm. But even the possibility of a vice president's role was not enough for Adil to reconsider his decision. In 1990, following the birth of his daughter, Nadia Mahnoor Khan, he decided to immigrate to Canada.

All that was left for Adil to do was convince his parents to undertake a second hijrat (migration) to the West, where his father had honed his skills and completed executive training programmes at renowned institutions like the Harvard University.

Adil recollected a conversation he had with the rest of his family members at the dinner table once. 'We already left Hyderabad once,' his mother bewailed, 'and now you are talking about having us leave Karachi for another place?' When travelling between India and Pakistan had not been so convoluted, Bilquis had really looked forward to her trips to Hyderabad. 'Why did we come here?' and 'We should have stayed there' were common laments ever since she had left her hometown.

But Adil had made up his mind. He borrowed $500 from his brother-in-law and sold a lot of his belongings to buy air tickets for himself, his wife and daughter, Nadia, who by then had turned one. His parents would follow soon. Anwar Ali had been offered the post of managing director by various government and corporate entities, but he, too, left for Canada with his wife on 1 September 1991.

The Great White North

Soon after landing in Canada, Adil got a job with Ontario Hydro (now Ontario Power Generation). There was already a bit of a Hyderabadi–Pakistani diaspora in Toronto, with several families having left Karachi to escape the violence and precariousness of daily life. Within four years of immigrating to Canada, Adil's son, Adnan Ali Khan, was born.

After working in different departments such as finance and IT at Ontario Power for twenty years, he joined an Indian company called I-Gate as an associate vice-president. With offices in Delhi, Hyderabad and Bangalore, the I-Gate job allowed him to travel back to his parents' hometown, where he still had some extended family.

One of the ways Adil remains connected to Hyderabad is through collecting art. His mother told him that his maternal grandfather Nawab Liaquat Jung Bahadur had the same hobby. 'He loved antiques. He owned a lot of clocks, watches and antique furniture. This hobby that became an obsession of sorts came about from my heritage and lineage,' he smiled.

During his trips to Hyderabad, Adil would often go to see the photographer Raja Deen Dayal's pictures at the Salar Jung Museum. Deen Dayal was the official photographer of the princely state. He had also taken photos of Adil's grandfather Liaquat Jung. Adil told me that these pictures also helped kindle his interest in art.

Bringing Glory to Hyderabad

'I want to do my part showcasing not just Hyderabad's but South Asia's art as well,' Adil stressed. This includes not only collecting works of artists from the subcontinent, but also ensuring that they get more visibility. Between 2020 and 2022, Adil donated over fifty paintings by Indian and Pakistani artists to the Royal Ontario Museum (ROM) in Toronto.

He also managed to convince ROM to acquire masterpieces by artists like Zain-ul-Abedin from Bangladesh, Pakistan's Sadequain and the Indian maestro Jamini Roy. Adil also showcased the work of Thota Vaikuntam, who uses paint and charcoal to skilfully recreate scenes of everyday life in rural Telangana.

The lack of representation for South Asian artists in Canada pushed Adil to establish the South Asian Gallery of Art. 'When I went to the

Art Gallery of Ontario, not a single piece by a South Asian or African artist could be seen anywhere. Some of these talented artists are told that their repertories are not "Canadian", he noted. In 2019, Adil and his son Adnan co-founded a not-for-profit called Shehla and Adil Giving for Art (SAGA) Foundation as a platform to promote South Asian art in Canada and abroad.

As Adil inches towards the end of his career, he plans to return to a company with a large carbon footprint—like Exxon—and lead its energy transition initiative. When the curtain draws on his career, he will focus just on art and his foundation.

A few months after Adil's father turned ninety, he died in the country that had become his third homeland. Three of Anwar's children are settled in the Toronto area. Asim, who was born in Hyderabad, Sindh, and is now New Jersey-based, has been a North American official of Imran Khan's Pakistan Tehreek-e-Insaaf party for several years.

Adil's children think of themselves as South Asian Canadian. Their connection to Hyderabad extends beyond a love for foods like biryani and tamatar ka kut (tomato curry with dried peppers and boiled eggs) or wearing attire like the sharara or the sherwani. Adnan and Mahnoor were taught how to read and write Urdu by their maternal grandmother.

'My son veers more towards the Bhopali part of his mixed South Asian heritage and my daughter is the Hyderabadi,' Khan said. His daughter, Mahnoor, now a Toronto-based surgeon, can instantly switch between the more standard Urdu and the informal Dakhani.

Whether it was uprooting themselves from Hyderabad or Karachi, the Ali family's journey is similar to that of many immigrant families from South Asia. Yet, like most Hyderabadi-Pakistanis with family in India in an era when video calling was non-existent, he lost touch with a lot of his Hyderabadi-Indian relatives.

As Adil and I approached the end of our conversation, Chef Baig brought us some khubani ka meetha (traditional Hyderabadi dessert made from fresh apricots) with crème brûlée. While we ate this fusion of French and Deccani cuisine, Khan showed me a little book he had brought with him. The book was titled *A Grand Father Figure: Mohammad Anwaruddin Ali.*

Kya Mumbai, Kya Karachi

The eighty-eight-page tribute that he put together for his father on his ninetieth birthday, begins with heartfelt birthday wishes from Anwar Ali's children, grandchildren and other relatives.

I was fascinated by the photographs of a young Anwar and scans of documents like his transfer certificate from the high school he attended in Gulbarga. But I was most intrigued by the penultimate section of the book, which contains a full chronology of Anwar's travels, starting from his move to Karachi in 1950 and ending with his trip to the same city in 2019.

His trips to Hyderabad from Karachi between 1953 and 1964 took me back to a time when it was easy to travel between the two countries. Although a visa system had been introduced in 1952, it was uncomplicated for citizens to obtain permits for family visits, pilgrimages and sporting events.[20] That was also a time when each country hosted branches of the banks of the other one.

Then, the 1965 War changed everything. Movement between the two countries became restricted. For the next fifty-five years, Anwar travelled to numerous other countries but he came to India only six times. He did not make it to Hyderabad on a majority of those trips, which were for business and strictly circumscribed by visa conditions that permitted him to only visit three cities.

Had it not been for both of our Canadian connections, I probably would not have had the chance to interact with Adil.

In most cases, neutral ground is the only way for Indians and Pakistanis to meet each other. These encounters are often devoid of the charge of politics and religion. At least in the diverse bubble of the gated community in which I grew up during my early years in Saudi Arabia (Chapter 3) the 1999 Kargil War or the aggressive rhetoric between the hawkish establishments of both countries did not have Indian and Pakistani expatriates at each other's throats.

My family used to often spend weekends at my paternal uncle's house in Jeddah's Mushrefah area, which was populated by many South Asian families. During one weekend in 1994, my uncle's Pakistani neighbours invited my cousins and me to watch the film *Karan Arjun* on a pirated VHS tape.

Yet, as the years passed by in Saudi, I eventually understood that there was no love lost between the two countries. But it took spending a year in the UK to understand how deeply entrenched the hostility was. In London, I came across several panels and protests sponsored by the intelligence agencies and embassies of both countries that painted the other in a negative light.

In Jeddah, I had met several of my Pakistani cousins. Like Mohammad Anwar Ali, many relatives of my parents had migrated to Pakistan at various points after Police Action. Growing up, I found it really interesting that some of these blood relatives sounded nothing like me or their grandparents, but rather like my other Pakistani and north Indian acquaintances. Once, I asked one of my Hyderabadi–Pakistani cousins, 'Do you consider yourself Indian or Pakistani?' 'Pakistani!' he had answered with patriotic zeal.

If any Hindi- or Urdu-speaking person had heard our conversation, they would think we belonged to two distinct cultures. Urdu purists would chuckle at my Dakhani accent. Hyderabadis would say that the Karachi/north Indian Urdu does not quite have the flavour that Telugu, Marathi and Kannada bring to Dakhani.

In North America, my accent is enough to nudge Pakistanis with ties to the Deccan towards the lanes of memory. These Hyderabadi–Pakistanis often tell me, 'I do not fully understand you, but my grandparents used to speak this hao-nakko Urdu you speak.'

I also noticed that some of my Hyderabadi-Pakistani relatives and acquaintances in North America are quite conflicted about their many identities. Some are at pains to distance themselves from Hyderabad and its manners as those sensibilities are equated with 'Indianness'. For others, their Pakistani identity sometimes leaves no room for expressions, cuisine or even attire from the Deccan.

Ali Adil Khan would never fall into this category. His conversation was sprinkled with haos and nakkos even as he mostly spoke the kind of Urdu I imagine is spoken on the streets of Karachi. I came away with the feeling that it would take only a week of immersion in Hyderabad city for him to sound like a local.

Before he left Baig's Grill, Khan gifted me the commemorative book he had compiled for his father. His parting words that afternoon reflected the tie that binds us across countries and continents: '*Kitaab rakh lo, miya! Kaam aayingi. Milingey Hyderabad mein shayad ek din apan!* (Keep the book, brother. You may find it useful. Maybe we will meet in Hyderabad some day!)'

Chukka Ramaiah: When Mathematics Met Marxism

اُٹھو میری دنیا کے غریبوں کو جگا دو

کاخِ امرا کے در و دیوار ہلا دو

—علامہ اقبال

Utho meri duniya ke ghareebon ko jaga do
Kaakh-e-umara ke dar-o-deewar hila do

Rise and awaken the poor of my world!
Tear down the walls and doors of the mansions of the great!

—Allama Iqbal

Telangana's Mangal Pandey

A man who was all of ninety-six years old sat behind a desk in the study of his Vidya Nagar home, which is not too far away from Osmania University. I sat before him along with his son Srinivas, who was visiting from San Francisco. The elderly person before me was Chukka Ramaiah, a well-known mathematics teacher, legislator and

112

sympathizer of the Left. And I was there to learn from him about a strand of Hyderabad history that is often buried within the narratives of Police Action—the Telangana Peasants' Rebellion.

'The Telangana Rebellion was never communal in character,' he asserted, 'It was a collective fight against the exploitative local landlords called doras, among whom were many Hindus.' To illustrate his point, he recalled the story of Sheikh Bandagi, a man referred to as Telangana's Mangal Pandey. Tales of Bandagi taking on a high-handed dora galvanized the communist rebellion that would engulf large parts of the Telangana countryside in the late 1940s.[1]

A farmer in the Kammareddy Gudem village of Warangal district, Bandagi had a dispute with his brother Abbas Ali about the equal division of their ancestral property. Ali took this matter to the local panchayat, over which the landlord, known as the dora, forcefully presided. Bandagi mobilized many farmers to support him in his battle against his brother and the oppressive landlord Ramachandra Reddy, who was also known as the Visnuru Deshmukh.

It took Bandagi three years to prevail. But Reddy was hungry for revenge. He turned Faqeer, a co-inheritor of the property in question, against Bandagi. This time, Reddy gamed the village courts, so that the decision would be in Faqeer's favour. Bandagi, revolting against the injustice, called on his supporters to reject every decision of the rural judiciary.

He also instituted a civil suit against Reddy in the local court. He finally won the case on 17 June 1941. During the time the matter was still ongoing, it was common for him to be on the receiving end of death threats and physical harassment from the dora's henchmen. His pride dented once again by the defeat in court, the dora felt he had to take drastic action. Thus, Visnuru Deshmukh sent his goons to murder Bandagi with knives and axes.

Chukka Ramaiah was a teenager when all this was playing out. Born in 1928 in the Gudur village of Nalgonda district, he had first-hand experience of the fervour inspired by Bandagi's crusade. He also grew up around a culture of exploitation and oppression in the farming economy. His difficulty in grasping the Urdu language drew him towards mathematics. And it was mathematics that helped him understand the ways in which landlords preyed on the villagers. After Police Action, he focused mainly on his teaching career for over the next forty years, apart from a term as a legislator from the teacher's constituency. But his empathy for the downtrodden and marginalized meant that he was constantly participating in progressive social movements.

Although Ramaiah's father had died of a paralytic stroke when he was fourteen years old, his mother wanted to see him educated and settled. But by then her son was already on the path to becoming a rebel, even though he had married a Telangana Brahmin girl in his mid-teenage years.

Hyderabad's Districts: Cesspools of Exploitation

'I studied in an Urdu-medium school mostly out of compulsion. Initially, it was very difficult to grasp. Back then, it was a bookish language to us; we used to speak Telugu in our households. I only wrote in Urdu but never spoke it much,' Ramaiah told me.

In Nizam-ruled Hyderabad, Urdu was the language of education and employment. The Asaf Jahi regime supported some vernacular schools and institutions,[2] but only Urdu could help young men land plum jobs in the civil administration and the military. Among the ruling elite, Telugu was seen as the language of the working classes.

At the time, the rural tracts of the Nizam's dominions were marked by a sinister kind of feudal oppression. The big landowners, known variously as jagirdars, doras or deshmukhs, treated their lower-caste labourers, peasantry and local citizens with disdain and tied them into vetti (a system of bonded labour). The hierarchy of the Asaf Jahi state meant that jagirdars and deshmukhs were often beholden to the

Paigahs, the high-ranking Muslim noblemen. The Nizam sat atop this hierarchy. This chain of tributes was a mighty weight on the labourers' backs as they toiled in fields of tobacco, castor seed, sesame, cotton and rice.

Gudur village, about 50 kilometres away from Warangal, was notorious for its rapacious moneylenders. Farmers would often borrow from them at exorbitant rates only to find themselves in a debt trap they could neither understand nor get out of. Growing up in an environment where farmers were bogged down by loans, concepts like simple and compound interest came easy to Ramaiah. They also helped him understand the dynamics of labour relations and moneylending. Now, as then, this web of exploitation is often underplayed by aristocratic families from Hyderabad city as well as the districts. It ruffles their idea of the Nizam's dominion as a beatific paradise, where their ancestors ruled with foresight and compassion for all of its citizenry.

The conditions were the opposite of benign when Chukka Ramaiah was growing up. Landowners were not above violence to keep peasants in check. Many of them had private armies at their disposal. To supplement this might, there was the local police. Communal lines were often blurred to ensure that the agrarian arrangement worked in favour of the landed and the nobles—Muslim militiamen were retained by landlords of the Reddy and Velma castes[3] to heavy-handedly quell any discontent brewing among the labourers.[4]

Something had to give. By the 1930s, there was an air of restiveness around rural Telangana. Peasants were no longer about to take the oppression inflicted upon them lying down. Soon enough, subversive ideas that had taken root in Russia would pose a challenge to this setup.

Reforms-cum-Regressive Measures

Although Salar Jung I's reign as princely Hyderabad's Prime Minister did see some positive reforms,[5] it also made life difficult for the population in the districts. Hindu landlords lost some of their power to collect revenue, but village officials known as patels and patwaris were given wide powers of taxation and punishment.[6] Salar Jung's administrative moves did not change the age-old dynamic between the doras and their labourers. The service castes continued to toil for them without remuneration and often in abysmal living conditions. The patwari may have been in-charge of revenue collection more directly, but no quarrel could be resolved in these tracts without the dora's involvement.[7]

With Hyderabad's economy being absorbed into a global one after World War I, the prices of crops were no longer influenced by the domestic supply and demand.[8] The Great Depression had diminished the value of agricultural exports.[9] The value of land depreciated and tenants' debts increased. The soaring rent, nonetheless, still had to be paid to the doras.[10]

However, things were about to change with the emergence of the Andhra Jana Sangham formed by the Telugu intelligentsia in 1921. In the context of this era, the term 'Andhra' signified an awareness of a common Telugu mother tongue.[11] Forty-eight years later, during the 1969 Telangana agitation, the term Andhra came to mean a specific region, and would be contrasted with the Telugu-speaking regions of Telangana. But back in the early 1920s, 'Andhra' had a linguistic and cultural connotation that pointed more broadly to the experience of Telugu-speakers in both the Madras Presidency and the Nizam's tracts.

By 1940, the Jana Sangham, which had by then evolved into the Andhra Mahasabha (AMS),[12] began mobilizing peasants against unequal structures and practices in the agrarian economy. The Communist Party of India (CPI) had been carrying out its work through the AMS[13] but come 1934, the CPI officially came into existence in Telugu areas of the Madras Presidency.[14]

AMS stalwarts like Puchalapalli Sundarayya visited several villages to propagate this awareness about tenant rights and promote Marxist teachings. The leader who later authored an authoritative memoir of this rebellion had gauged that Ramaiah was a well-spoken, energetic and conscious youngster who had a way with numbers.

Telangana Peasants' Rebellion

The movement that began in the 1920s with the Jana Sangham expanded to over 3,000 villages and ended up affecting three million people. Although the Razakars were out to defend the 'Muslim' state throughout Hyderabad, they were also drafted to uphold the supremacy of the Hindu doras in the Telangana region.[15]

To combat the landlords who allowed the Majlis Ittehad-ul-Muslimeen's militia to establish camps in their estates, the peasantry had been organized into different village sangams (collectives that were offshoots of the AMS) and conferences to help abolish taxation and vetti (bonded labour).[16]

Just when the Telangana Rebellion became an armed struggle, Ramaiah got caught in 1946 and spent two years in the Aurangabad jail. While he was in jail, a kind prison attendant, whose daughter Ramaiah had helped with Telugu and mathematics lessons, asked him about the type of books he read. When he answered that he mostly read mathematical textbooks and Marxist literature, he was nudged towards more general books. Among the works he was given were *The Discovery of India, Letters from a Father to His Daughter* and a collection of booklets containing Pandit Motilal Nehru's speeches. Ramaiah told me that his English improved drastically by reading these books.

By 1947, armed peasants in the Warangal, Nalgonda and Mahabubnagar districts had been successful in ousting many doras and deshmukhs from their fiefdoms. On the eve of Police Action in September, large swathes of Telangana were being run by nominally independent village communes called gram rajyams. After the Indian military ousted the Nizam, they turned their attention to the communists.

Due to those gains made by the guerrillas, Deputy Prime Minister Sardar Vallabhbhai Patel knew that Indian troops needed to make their way to Hyderabad—first to merge the princely state into the union and then to crush the communists who were growing stronger by the day.[17] Prime Minister Jawaharlal Nehru, too, was weary of the growing influence of the Left. Thus, after Police Action, he stressed the need for a healing touch to disenfranchised Muslims so as to prevent them from leaning towards the leftist factions.[18] This healing touch was also for peasants because many Congress members understood why they gravitated towards the leftist contingencies who addressed their grievances.[19]

Nonetheless, some within the party brass regarded Nehru's Congress as a sworn enemy with whom there could be no rapprochement.

Calling Off the Armed Struggle

In February 1948, the CPI held its second congress, where its general secretary, B.T. Ranadive, declared India's Independence a sham, while pushing for the Telangana Armed Struggle to continue.

According to the well-known leftist activist Burgula Narsing Rao, who also participated in the Telangana Peasants' Rebellion, to cement relations with China's Maoist regime, Andhra leaders like Sundarayya and Satyanarayana seconded Ranadive. They did not have a high opinion of Nehru, whom they believed to be a lackey of Anglo-American imperialism.[20] But down south, the armed conflict between leftist guerrillas and the Indian forces raged on.

Peasants, students, villagers and party workers who formed mobile guerrilla squads were no match for the more organized, experienced Indian military. There were also stories of barbarism coming from the districts. Not only did soldiers place heavy stones upon the bodies of villagers, they also stepped on them with nailed boots.[21] Instances of rape were aplenty.[22]

Fortunately for those in the districts of Telangana, Ajoy Ghosh, Ranadive's successor as general secretary of the CPI, put the party on a path that would ultimately have it transition into parliamentary politics, much to the dismay of the Andhra region's party provincial committee (PC). The lack of consensus among the Andhra PC and other CPI contingents about the future of the insurrection prompted the leadership to defer the final decision to the Cominform and Joseph Stalin.

Key Communist Party members—Ajoy Ghosh, S.A. Dange, Rajeshwar Rao and Makineni Basavapunnaiah—were dispatched to Moscow. Stalin declared that nothing could come out of a campaign that was limited to less than five districts of Hyderabad state. Since Russia wanted to establish fraternal relations with India, he encouraged them to drop the rhetoric of Nehru being an Anglo-American stooge. To Stalin, Indian communists would be wise to further their cause through electoral politics, as their French and Italian counterparts were doing.[23]

The armed struggle was called off by October 1951,[24] especially in light of the casualties that had been piling up. The damages from the protracted war between the Indian military and the communists were substantial: 4,000 killed; 10,000 jailed.[25] To weed out the revolutionaries, the Reddy and Velma doras had guided the Indian Army through their old stomping grounds.[26] The Muslim gentry may have lost their moorings after Police Action, but Telangana's Hindu nobility had their fiefdoms restored after the Indian military quelled the insurrection and the communists put down their weapons.

The victory against the landlords was short-lived as they were now a part of the Congress establishment.

Starting Afresh

Ramaiah had been released from prison in 1948. Before, during and after his two-year sentence, his family continued to be ostracized because of his revolutionary activities. Some extended family members were land revenue officials—their livelihoods had been disrupted by the peasants' rebellion. Ramaiah's habit of freely fraternizing with communists as well as lower-caste folk was another reason he was alienated by his extended family and acquaintances.

Luckily, around that time Ramaiah had a guardian of sorts in prominent public prosecutor and relative from Warangal, Venkat Ramaiah. Not only did Venkat provide some financial security, he helped facilitate the marriage of one of Ramaiah's elder sisters.

Except, getting released from prison was just the first step in starting a new life. Only Ramaiah's mother stood by him when he was ostracized due to his police record and his mingling with the Dalits. He never picked up arms during the days of the rebellion but it was still hard for him to adjust to normal life. He was someone who followed the ideals of Russian socialist writer Maxim Gorky and read aloud his works to fellow villagers. He also very much sympathized with the continued armed rebellion.

Srinivas attested, 'Of course, tutoring the superintendent's daughter put him in the good books of various prison personnel, but his caste identity came in handy in and outside of prison, especially when he needed a clean record after his rebellious activities.' His renowned comrades Raj Bahadur Gour, Makhdoom Mohiuddin, Arutla Ramachandra Reddy and Dharma Bhiksham advised Ramaiah that as a literate person, it was more worthwhile for him to finish his education and work as a teacher rather than volunteer full-time for the party. At their urging, he went to college to get an undergraduate degree.

After his studies, he was keen to find a job. This in itself was a challenging task for anyone who had been associated with the communists. 'He was told to speak to a central government administrator or a principal secretary who happened to be of my father's community,' Srinivas told me, 'The highly placed officer wrote on the back of a cigarette pack "Give Ramaiah a job".'

In 1951, he landed a job as a teacher in a government school in rural Telangana. With Urdu no longer the government language, Telugu was receiving more patronage than before.

'When the Telugu language became a medium of instruction in 1950, it was a boon for us,' Ramaiah said. 'Because of that, more learning took place; and during that year, twelve out of forty students got first class. When Urdu had been prevalent, many students used to just copy or memorize everything from the textbook. The Telugu-medium education helped sharpen our thinking.'

Telugu would get more of a fillip once the state of Andhra Pradesh would be formed in 1956. The idea of a unified Telugu state had a bit of a history. As early as 1941, the Communist Party, under the banner of the Andhra Mahasabha, had envisioned an entity they called 'Vishalandhra', which would bring together the Telugu-speakers of the Nizam's dominions and the Madras Presidency. Ramaiah was a major supporter of this concept.

The Mulki agitation, a precursor to the first struggle for a separate Telangana state, took off just as Ramaiah began what would become a prolific teaching career. After people from the Madras Presidency were brought in to fill jobs in academia and bureaucracy, protests erupted throughout the state.

The Mulki Movement

Many denizens of Telangana resented the influx of Telugu-speakers from the erstwhile Madras Presidency regions. The disgruntled population cut across linguistic and social groups of the old Nizam's dominions. Muslims, Kayasthas and Telugu-speakers all stressed upon how different Telangana's culture was from the manners of the 'non-Mulkis'. They deplored the economic and social domination they also faced at the hands of the 'non-Mulki' elite.

Ramaiah had a different view. He felt that the Telangana region had benefited from the migration of Andhraites. 'Many Telugu-speaking Andhraite teachers who had come from the Madras Presidency helped uplift a lot of the Hyderabad and Telangana region's students,' he remembered, 'These were students for whom education had been inaccessible because they were not learning in their native language. Sometimes, they were too poor to pursue studies.'

Numerous teachers who came from Andhra were of the leftist persuasion, which enabled Ramaiah to build a union movement. But this did not blind him from the fact that Andhra's political and commercial class were increasingly calling the shots in the state. What he found more distressing was that the feudal lords of rural Telangana, whom he had fought tooth and nail against, had their dominions restored after ingratiating themselves to the new Congress establishment.

When these developments were occupying the mind-space of Ramaiah, his old comrade Raj Bahadur Gour insisted he focus on the quotidian. Gour, who hosted many nomadic comrades, stressed that he would realize the value of owning a home when he would have his own family. He not only advised Ramaiah to buy a house, but he helped him do so.

When cries for a new state got louder, Chukka Ramaiah would not heed them. He had decided to focus on his family, his profession and getting a master's degree. Between 1952 and 1967, he earned his living by teaching in government schools in different districts. After getting wind of his gifts as a teacher, bureaucrats who were stationed at the places he taught often sought him out to tutor their children.

Srinivas, his oldest child, was born in 1962 in a house that Ramaiah had bought in Vidya Nagar Colony of Hyderabad city.

Steering Clear of the First Push for a Separate State

Srinivas was a young boy when the 1969 Telangana agitation took place. Students took to the streets, protesting against government jobs being taken by those who were not from Telangana. The grouse had been festering for several years though, starting from the Mulki agitation of 1952. At the time of the states' linguistic reorganization in 1956, there had been the Gentlemen's Agreement between the regions, with the Andhra party pledging that there would be no discrimination against Telangana regarding jobs and government expenditures.

As an elementary school student, Srinivas remembered protestors burning exam papers at his school in Nallakunta. On the road leading to OU, where his father was pursuing his MSc in mathematics, people would pelt stones. He told me that the first push for statehood did not have the mass character of the one that would be successful five decades later. The 1969 campaign was more centred on employment rights for the Mulkis.

Ramaiah did clarify that he had immense respect for some of the people who were at the forefront of the agitation, but he differed from them ideologically. Some of these leaders included K.R. Amos, who was the founding president of the Non-Gazetted Officers' Union; Professor Keshav Rao Jadhav, the head of the Osmania University Teachers' Association; and academic Kothapalli Jayashankar. 'If Telangana came into being after 1969, the landed gentry many of us leftists fought against would once again reign supreme,' added Ramaiah.

As a union member, he mobilized and helped strengthen the State Teachers' Union, which was inclined towards the left. Ramaiah was aware of the concerns that teachers in the Telangana region had. For him, being a good and sincere teacher in the classroom was enough to lend credibility and public support for the teachers' movement.

Becoming Politically Aware

'From 1972, my father emphasized two things: maths and progressive politics,' Srinivas said. 'He introduced me to Sundarayya's books and lessons. I heard about figures like CPI leader Nalla Narasimhulu. And of course, he told me about the legendary Makhdoom Mohiuddin,' he continued.

Having obtained his MSc as a gold medallist and private student at the age of forty, Ramaiah got his first job as a mathematics lecturer in a government degree college in OU. In 1970, he set off for Siddipet, where he helped set up the Siddipet Government Colleges Teachers' Association. Achut, Srinivas's younger brother, was born in 1982.

Ramaiah won many admirers in this town that is about 100 kilometres north of Hyderabad, not least because of the courageous stances he took on behalf of students and against the management. But his uncompromising approach to principles and ethical conduct also made him some enemies—many in the student body who did not appreciate Ramaiah's stand against cheating.

The family stayed in Hyderabad. They went to Siddipet and later on to Nalgonda for the summer holidays, where they shared their father's home with children from different villages. It was also where Srinivas and his siblings received their political education. Interactions with people from diverse backgrounds broadened their worldview.

In 1979, Srinivas joined OU to study electrical engineering. 'However, my left-oriented politics were different compared to the very urban crowd that usually studied in my stream of engineering,' he differentiated. Srinivas was on campus at the time when progressive movements inspired by activist Cyril Reddy took forward the idealism of his brother, George.

OU always had a legacy of progressive politics, ever since the 1930s, but in the shadow of the Naxalbari uprising in the late 1960s, the movement had taken a more decisive turn towards the left.[27] The dynamic OU campus was where Telangana folk singer Gaddar raised consciousness and groups like the Andhra Pradesh Radical Students' Union emerged.[28] Through the Gramalaku Taralandi campaign, these groups took the students to the villages of Telangana to spread the message of agrarian revolution.

Srinivas had another intellectual idol in human rights activist Kandala Balagopal. When I asked if he ever considered the path taken by Balagopal or his father, he responded, 'I very much got a political education. But I doubt I had the dedication and commitment to sustain a career as a political activist. I did not have the calibre and depth of experience that my father possesses.'

Meanwhile, his father was faced with a crossroads in his own life. In 1983, Chief Minister N.T. Rama Rao suddenly decreased the retirement age from fifty-eight to fifty-five.[29] At a time when the private sector was non-existent, this ended up limiting Ramaiah's employment options.

The Communist Party of India-Marxist (CPI-M) gave him two choices: either join the party full-time at a wage of Rs 500 to Rs 600 per month; or contest the Member of Legislative Council election from Warangal on a teacher's ticket. He opted for the second route, but was defeated in the polls.

The family got by, but they were not financially stable then. One of Srinivas's sisters started to work at the Electronics Corporation of India, while the other was still pursuing an undergraduate degree. His youngest brother was in middle school at the time. Their father did not foresee nor desire political careers for his children. 'He wanted me to help out with running the family and be a role model for my siblings by putting my education and career first,' Srinivas said.

To the Land of Opportunity

In 1985, Srinivas went to Texas to pursue his PhD in electrical engineering. Financial circumstances prompted Ramaiah to start a coaching class with fellow teachers, G. Madhusudhan Rao and B. Surendranath Reddy. They taught school and college students, while also preparing aspirants for the Joint Entrance Exam of the prestigious Indian Institutes of Technology. The classes took off, with students flocking to this combination of teachers who were excellent at explaining fundamental concepts of math and science.

A few years later, on the other side of the world, Srinivas completed his PhD and secured a job as a scientist at GE Research in upstate New York. Srinivas's sisters got married, earned graduate degrees and settled in the US as well. Achut, too, would move to the US after completing his degree at IIT Roorkee.

Srinivas got married in 1992 and then moved to Boston. Despite being far away from home, he continued to express his opinion on Indian issues like the demolition of Babri Masjid. He did this on chat rooms and other online forums, where he was active along with other Non-Resident Indians (NRIs). There used to be intense debates on Andhra-specific issues too. Srinivas told me he remembered debating farmers' suicides and arguing against the economic policies of Chandrababu Naidu.

Eventually, he moved out west to San Francisco.

Beyond the Binary

Expectedly, when the Telangana statehood issue began to heat up in the late 2000s and early 2010s, Srinivas kept himself informed about those developments. His own view of the issue was similar to his father, who had never viewed it through an 'us versus them' lens. 'Never have I bought into this rhetoric that every single Andhraite in Telangana is out to exploit me,' he stressed, 'I would prefer a Sundarayya-esque personality than any heavy-handed landlord-type statesman from Andhra or Telangana as a public representative. As someone who left the country thirty years ago, my ordinary friends hailing from Vijayawada, Nellore and various cities are more embedded in Hyderabad city's soil than I am.'

In 2007, Ramaiah was elected as a Member of Legislative Congress (MLC) on a ticket provided by the United Teachers Front, which was affiliated with the CPI-M. During his six years as MLC, he shed light on the Andhra political establishment's partiality to concentrate infrastructural development mostly in Hyderabad city and claim ownership thereof. Ramaiah also spoke out against the irrigational and educational resource allocation to the state's coastal district elite interests at the expense of the overall Telangana region.

Srinivas accepted that there was a certain type of Andhra politician and businessman who was unscrupulous, but that did not mean that the entire debate had to be cast in the 'native versus outsider' terms that was gaining currency among politicians and ordinary citizens. The broader issue was how the needs of underdeveloped regions get unfairly deprioritized to that of dominant elite from the developed regions. In many instances, Srinivas made it clear that the simplistic binary may not translate into an egalitarian struggle for justice, fairness and equal development of all, but also could be an excuse for Telangana-based dominant castes and real estate lobbies to displace builders and landowners from Andhra. During the Telugu Desam Party (TDP) and Congress regimes, many proponents of statehood were accused of harbouring ulterior motives to gain possession of land that was earlier owned by the Nizams but was now taken over by politicians and builders from Andhra.[30]

There is some truth to the fact that the advent of the TDP had changed the cultural, economic and political landscape of Telangana. The region came to be increasingly dominated by the landed elite from Coastal Andhra. Telanganites who owned vast tracts of land in the Ranga Reddy district had sold them to the landowning communities from the Andhra region for hefty amounts.

NTR's reign was not just about taking over the crown lands. Schedule V lands that were specifically allocated for Scheduled Tribes (ST) were not spared either.[31] The ST lands in the Khammam, Warangal, Karimnagar and Adilabad districts were for the taking. Things did not improve when Chandrababu Naidu, NTR's son-in-law, took over the TDP. The real estate and software booms might have painted a picture of a vibrant economy, but the land in Andhra Pradesh was still controlled by a small, ruling elite. Many rural tracts owned by small farmers were taken over by private and public interests after bribing the panchayat to pass resolutions in their favour.[32]

Besides, there was a further erosion of Telangana's distinct culture. When the Telugu film industry shifted base from Chennai to Hyderabad, caricatures of the Telangana dialect and culture became more common. Characters from the region were depicted as silly comedians or goofy villains. In all cases, their Urdu-, Marathi- and Kannada-influenced Telugu was presented as an object of ridicule and uncouthness.

Another major issue was the unequal distribution of water resources between the three main regions of united Andhra Pradesh: Coastal Andhra, Telangana and Rayalaseema. 'The Coastal Andhra elite sought a very one-sided distribution,' Srinivas pointed out.

This is borne out by reports from the 1980s onwards. The TDP, which was dominated by functionaries from Coastal Andhra, formed a committee to evaluate the surplus flows in the Krishna river only after an agitation by the Rayalaseema leadership.

Upon the committee identifying 200 to 300 TMC (trillion million cubic) feet, 30 TMC feet were then allocated to the Srisailam Left Bank Canal (SLBC) project. Proposed as a gravity canal that would terminate at the Moosi river, Telangana's drought-prone Nalgonda district stood to benefit from the SLBC. The committee also designated funds for the Srisailam Right Branch, which today irrigates many districts in the Rayalaseema region. When it came to taking forward and funding the SLBC, both the TDP and Congress governments dragged their feet.[33]

Despite these imbalances in the 1980s, Ramaiah still did not see the merits of a new state. But as the injustices became more glaring through the 1990s, he warmed up to the idea of bifurcation. Many of his leftist compatriots still balked at the thought of a separate state. But he came to understand that the statehood struggle was a just and progressive cause that would only benefit the people of Telangana. However, at the same time he constantly reminded those who undertook the campaign with him that the push for bifurcation was not against the common people of the three regions that made up Andhra Pradesh.

Ramaiah was asked to be the convenor of the Telangana Joint Action Committee (JAC) that had supplemented the Telangana

Rashtra Samithi party's efforts during the agitation. He refused citing his age. Instead, Professor Kodandram took charge of the JAC in 2009.

In 2011, the JAC organized the Million March protest, which brought together people from several pro-statehood groups. As part of the agitation, statues of many Telugu icons were uprooted in the Tankbund area of Hyderabad city. The statues left untouched were of Rani Rudrama Devi, the last ruler of Telangana's Kakatiya dynasty, and the Qutub Shahi monarch Abul Hasan Tana Shah.[34]

While Ramaiah did not participate in the march, he addressed students staging protests and demonstrations at OU and other higher learning institutions. Once, he was arrested for trying to enter the Osmania campus to express solidarity with a student-led protest.[35] When the bifurcation did take place in 2014, it did not allay Ramaiah's fears of the feudal elite still holding sway over the state. While the barons from Coastal Andhra still remained, they were now working together with Telangana's landed contingents, who had achieved fresh political and commercial clout in the separate state.[36]

This is not the only fault line in the state today. A distinct religious polarization has begun to make its presence felt in Telangana.

Rekindling of the 'Exploiter Versus Exploited' Dynamic

Srinivas told me about a time when some Hindu Mahasabha activists came to the villages in the 1940s. '"We Hindus should be united and fight against the Nizams and Razakars"—that is what they used to say.' His father then completed the story. 'Yes. The Razakars and the Nizam were problematic. But it would be wrong to not look at the local Hindu landlord as a guilty party too.' Ramaiah repeated, 'The Telangana Rebellion had a secular and not a communal character—as Muslims like Bandagi inspired us to stand up against cruel landlords.'

Srinivas then talked about Hussain, a neighbourhood tailor in their Vidya Nagar locality.

'His family has been there since my grandparents' time, and I greet him every day when I am here. We are always delighted to hear about how well his son is doing in Saudi Arabia. These interactions and my conversations with the different types of people my father used to bring home have made me immune to the notion of the "ghetto Muslim", so I can stand up against the Hindutva rhetoric.'

Srinivas has tried to pass on this egalitarian line of thinking to his children, who are American citizens. They have even gone to protests together. As a family, they took interest in human rights issues from time to time. They also joined many other Indian-Americans in protesting the life imprisonment of civil rights activist Binayak Sen, who allegedly helped Maoist guerrillas. Srinivas's son, who is currently a student at the Harvard Medical School, co-authored an article in *The Scientific American* about healthcare for Palestinian children.

They are very much of the Bernie Sanders persuasion. Even Srinivas's younger Virginia-based brother, Achut, attributes his support for Sanders to the empathy and social consciousness that was in the air of their homes during their formative years. The context of Srinivas's and Achut's lives might be far removed from their father's, especially when he started his political activism during a peasants' rebellion in rural Telangana. But, in thought and deed, they seem to have learnt from his long journey of seeing the essential and common humanity of one and all as they walk along with the powerless and the disenfranchised.

Apparasu Srinivasa Rao: '*Yadundi Telangana?*'

او چنا ریڈّی ماما! ویر ایز تلنگانہ؟
— گلی نلگونڈوی

Oh Chenna Reddy Mama! Where is Telangana?

—Gilli Nalgondvi

'My Mother Cried When Huzoor Nizam Surrendered'

On 16 September 2021, Siasat.com published a personal piece by the journalist Apparasu Srinivasa Rao, known as ASR in Hyderabad's media circles. The article was titled 'My Mother Cried When Huzoor Nizam Surrendered to the Indian Army'. The headline was striking because it reflected an ostensible anomaly—a Telugu-speaking Hindu woman saddened by the integration of a Muslim-ruled princely state into the secular, democratic republic of India.

The article detailed his mother Sampathamma's account of life under the rule of Mir Osman Ali Khan, the last Nizam. She mentioned the lack of a communal temperament in Alaa Hazrat, who

131

treated his Hindu and Muslim employees equally. She remarked on his generosity towards government officers, which contrasted with the many legends about his miserliness. His 'bad name', she felt, was precipitated by the emergence of the Razakars, who used to 'roam around the streets to kill the Hindus indiscriminately'. In her telling, the Nizam was helpless in the face of this violence. Sampathamma also recalled the high standard of cleanliness in Hyderabad city under the Nizam's reign.

ASR, who was born in 1964, would be baffled by these tales of the old days. In the Siasat.com article, he wrote that his own idea about the Nizam's rule was less than charitable. It had been informed by Telugu films like *Maa-bhoomi* and *Chillara Devullu*, which portrayed how callously peasants had been treated in the feudal system that was an enduring feature of Asaf Jahi rule.

It was not as though Sampathamma had blinkers on about the abysmal conditions in rural Telangana. After all, Apparasu Sheshagiri Rao, her husband, was a communist who had thrown in his lot with Makhdoom Mohiuddin, the poet-scholar who played an active role in the peasants' uprising that engulfed the countryside. The target of that rebellion was first the princely state of the Asaf Jahi dynasty and then the Indian Republic.

After the armed rebellion had been called off, there were other battles, too. Despite being directly affected by migration from Andhra in the wake of the states' reorganization in 1956, Sheshagiri Rao remained indifferent to the first agitation for a Telangana state in 1969. But, decades later, his son, daughter-in-law and grandchildren would resist—in their own way—what they saw as the hegemony of the Andhra establishment.

These were the tales I heard from ASR. In 2021, when the second wave of the Covid-19 pandemic began to subside, we connected a few times over Zoom and email.

Sampathamma died in mid-2023. When I met her granddaughter, Sruthi, back in late 2020, she had told me about the traces of Urdu in the Telugu her grandmother spoke. For instance, mukhtasari, the Teluguized-form of the Urdu word mukhtasar (brief), had been a part of her parlance. After 1956, this dialect had gradually been diluted by a more purist version of Telugu.[1]

And so begins another generational story that cannot be contained within the confines of the binary narratives of mainstream Hyderabadi history. The Rao family's story, too, has a strong communist strand, but its shade is different from Chukka Ramaiah's narrative in the previous chapter. This was a city-bred family, whose many members were part of the Nizam's establishment and had first-hand experience of his benevolence. Even as Sheshagiri Rao railed against the unjust exploitation in the feudal tracts of Telangana, he never said a mean word about the Asaf Jahi dynasty—in contrast to some of his comrades and the literature he was exposed to.

Life in Hyderabad Under the Nizam's Rule

The Brahmins and Kayasthas were an integral part of the finance and revenue departments in princely Hyderabad. One such bureaucrat in the Mehkama-e-Aabkari, the excise department, was ASR's paternal grandfather Apparasu Narasimha Rao. His brother, Apparasu Ranga Rao, also worked for the Nizam's administration, as a deputy tehsildar (revenue officer). They lived in the Hari Bowli neighbourhood of Mughalpura in the Old City.

Like many Hindu government employees in Nizam-ruled Hyderabad, Narasimha Rao was a polyglot. But his talent and interest in literary matters stood out from the rest. His poems can be found in *Golconda Kavula Sanchika*, a Telugu poetry collection compiled by historian Suravaram Pratap Reddy. Narasimha Rao was also a Sanskrit scholar. With the Muslim nobles who visited him at his home and workplace he spoke flawless Urdu. Fluency in Urdu, alongside their mother tongues of Kannada, Telugu or Marathi, was not out of the ordinary for many Hindu residents of Nizam-ruled Hyderabad.

Burgula Ramakrishna Rao, the second chief minister of Hyderabad state, for instance, spoke Urdu, English, Hindi, Sanskrit, Arabic and Persian, alongside his native Telugu.

Narasimha Rao was unlike other Hyderabadi bureaucrats in at least one other way: he happily took up postings outside Hyderabad city, which the others sought to avoid. By the end of his career, he had served in places like Parbhani, Aurangabad, Makhtal, Kollapur and Nizamabad.

Unlike Chukka Ramaiah (Chapter 7), who had spent his early years in rural Telangana, Sheshagiri Rao had grown up amidst the urban comforts of Hyderabad city. ASR's father may not have had a personal axe to grind against Osman Ali Khan. Yet, when it came to taking a stand against the exploitative system that the Asaf Jahi regime presided over, he was no less rebellious than Ramaiah.

A Household Rebel

In the Hyderabad of the 1930s, the Marxist ideology had found takers among college students. Youngsters like Burgula Narsing Rao and Raj Bahadur Gour had initially gravitated towards Gandhian ideals. But soon, they felt that communism would be better suited to topple the feudal structures of the Nizam-ruled state.

Osmania University was a hotbed of this movement. A number of professors there had earned their degrees from British institutions where Marxist thought was in vogue. The writings of socialists like Sidney and Beatrice Webb were all the rage. During his time at OU, Sheshagiri Rao's interest in Urdu poetry had brought him close to Makhdoom Mohiuddin, who was at the forefront of the trade union movement in Hyderabad.

Makhdoom's day job was that of an Urdu lecturer in City College. He had already made a name for himself by then. At OU, where he had come to study from the small town of Medak, he attracted several admirers for his ability to turn a verse. In 1940, he became one of the first members of the Hyderabad city chapter of the Communist Party.[2] At City College, students waited to hear him recite his newest compositions or hold forth on domestic and international politics.

After resigning from his job to focus on party and union activities, Makhdoom would organize 'communist classes' and literary gatherings. Sheshagiri Rao's political awakening came during these sessions.

His son recounted an interesting story to me about a Makhdoom poem titled 'Chaara-gar'. The musical rendition of this poem, known as *'Ek Chameli Ke Mandve Tale'*, is still a staple at ghazal parties in the households of old Hyderabadi families. 'Chaara-gar' was one of Makhdoom's less politically charged and more romantic poems. When Sheshagiri Rao once started reciting it, he was hit on the head by Makhdoom, who then admonished him for singing romantic songs in 'communist class'.

An Adventurous Messenger

The efforts of the Communist Party to challenge Hyderabad's feudal establishment began to pay off. In many places, peasants were resisting the exploitation of landlords, revenue officials and Razakars. Communist youth who came from elite, urban families began to believe that a revolution akin to Russia's was imminent. The British authorities were tracking the developments with increasing alarm. In 1946, as the Telangana Rebellion became an armed struggle, the Communist Party was banned.

Large tracts of the countryside came to be taken over by village communes. The communists' call had been to convert dora rajyam, the rule of landlords, to praja rajyam, the rule of the people. But these victories were short-lived. In September 1948, the Indian military operation ran roughshod over the Nizam's army. Operation Polo was completed in five days. At the time, Sampathamma, who would be married to Sheshagiri Rao in two years, was eleven years old. On

17 September 1948, her family was crowded around a radio set at their Aliabad residence in the Old City. They heard the Nizam announce—in Dakhani—that he was stepping down and that Hyderabad state would merge with the Indian Union. At the end of the speech, all of them burst into tears and wept for a long time. Seventy-three years later, this is the moment that Sampathamma's son would write about in an article for Siasat.com.

After the completion of the annexation, the army turned its attention to extinguishing the communist influence that had taken root in the countryside. Leftists, young and old, would go underground during this period. Many of them would elude the Indian authorities for another three years.

During this period, a young Sheshagiri Rao carried secret messages for the party. 'A little drop box had been hidden inside a lamp post in the Old City for messages,' ASR told me. 'My father was told to scribble a coded message given by a prominent party member and then keep the slip in the lamp post. This slip would then be picked up by civil rights activist and poet M.T. Khan, who would pass on the message to another intermediary.' For a long time, Sheshagiri Rao did not know that many of these messages originated from and were meant for Makhdoom, who was on the run then.

ASR told me another couple of anecdotes from this period. Puchalapalli Sundarayya, the Andhra Mahasabha leader who was underground from 1948 to 1952, once spent a day at Sheshagiri Rao's Old City residence. ASR's uncle Shyamsdundar Rao had told him how his adventurous brother once dropped an on-the-run Tarimela Nagi Reddy to the railway station on his bicycle. Reddy, a prominent communist from Andhra, would go on to become a member of Parliament and a member of Andhra Pradesh's Legislative Assembly.

As the Indian Army began making further inroads into the Telangana districts, Sheshagiri Rao was compelled to go into hiding in a village on the border of Warangal district and the Madras Presidency.

The Distant Observer

Sheshagiri Rao disassociated himself from the party after the Peasants' Rebellion petered out in 1951. The party brass had been advised by Stalin to emerge overground and contest elections in India. Prime Minister Nehru, too, had sought rapprochement with Hyderabad state's communist factions by releasing many of their prisoners.

Unlike his guru Makhdoom, Sheshagiri Rao did not dive into electoral politics. Nor did he continue to carry out union activities, as Chukka Ramaiah did in government colleges. Makhdoom's former courier turned his attention to making ends meet by trying his hand at various vocations—these included farming in his native village of Vinjamur, marketing bicycle seats for a period and working as a village patwari (registrar or accountant). He spent his leisure time reading instalments of the *Jasoosi Dunya* detective series, authored by Ibn-e-Safi. He also attended the frequent literary gatherings at Makhdoom's residence.

In the 1960s, Sheshagiri Rao settled into a job at the AP State Cooperative Union in the Gunfoundry area of Hyderabad city. It had been a few years since a unified Andhra Pradesh came into existence. By this time, the fissures between people from Andhra and Telangana had started deepening.

The early fault lines went back to 1951, when people from Telangana started resisting what they saw as the overrepresentation of Andhraites in the government and education sectors. Potti Sriramulu had died from a hunger strike while demanding a unified state, one that Madras Presidency's Telugu-speaking population could call its own. He got his wish in death, even as people like Burgula Ramakrishna Rao had expressed their apprehension about Telugus from Andhra state dominating the Telugus from Telangana.

The Gentlemen's Agreement had been signed by Andhra and Telangana representatives at the time of states' reorganization, but violations of it continued unabated well into the 1960s. It was suggested (even by Sampathamma) that officials who were from Telangana had taken bribes from Andhra migrants in exchange for issuing domicile or 'Mulki' certificates.

All this culminated in the unsuccessful agitation for a separate state in 1969. Like Abid Ali Khan (Chapter 1) and Chukka Ramaiah (Chapter 7), Sheshagiri Rao steered clear of the struggle. 'My father never disclosed his feelings about Andhra domination or the bifurcation, but he was a keen observer of contemporary politics,' stated ASR. His father also remained indifferent towards Marri Chenna Reddy and Ananthula Madan Mohan—leaders of the movement.

ASR, who was born in Nagarkurnool five years before the 1969 agitation, where his father had been posted, further clarified, 'Interestingly enough, my father did not like it when the Telangana Praja Samithi, which was fighting tooth and nail for the separate state, merged with the Congress in 1971. Yet, he never openly endorsed the Telangana campaign.'

Jai Telangana, ca. 1969

ASR told me that the careers of both his father and grandfather had been adversely affected by the dominance of Telugu-speakers from the erstwhile Madras Presidency. He elaborated, 'I was told my grandfather could have retired as excise superintendent, but the prevalence of Andhra employees, who had a hold on many departments and their top posts, had rendered that position out of reach.'

ASR had also been told by elders that Andhraites had cornered the plum postings in the city at the expense of Mulkis, who were dispatched to remote places. His father, who eventually went on to become a district cooperative educational instructor, had been ignored for a promotion to zonal education officer due to the domination of those from Rayalaseema and Coastal Andhra regions. As a result, his children had to be sent to government schools. ASR would receive his schooling at the Government Upper Primary School in Kalwagadda and then at the Kayastha-founded Dharamwant High School in Yaqutpura.

However, Sheshagiri Rao's brother and some of his cousins had taken a different route. Shyamsundar Rao had played an active role in the movement to demand a fair treatment for Telangana since the Mulki protests of the early 1950s. He was involved in the 1969 agitation for separate statehood. Although initially a part of the CPI mould, which believed in the idea of 'Vishalandhra', a united Telugu state, he then had a change of heart. For playing his part in the first push for Telangana, he even served a brief jail term in Mahabubnagar. The pro-Vishalandhra turned pro-statehood activist went on to become a state member of the Legislative Council from the teachers' constituency on behalf of the CPI-affiliated State Teachers' Union.

The Ramiza Bi Riots

When I asked ASR about what he thought of the religious fault lines in Hyderabad, he told me that he had grown up in an era that was not as communally charged. He grew up in the Lal Darwaza–Aliabad areas, which was known for fraternal relations between Hindus and Muslims.

When the mood of the city transformed after the Ramiza Bi riots in 1978, ASR was in Warangal, where his father had been posted. That was when the Old City was placed under curfew for a total of about fifty days,[3] over three instances of violence. Ramiza Bi was a Muslim woman who had been sexually assaulted by police officers for filing a complaint against the law enforcement officials who killed her husband. The resulting riots led to the first of many communal-linked curfews that would be imposed on the city over the next few years.

'During my childhood, I never heard of such occurrences in the Lal Darwaza or Shah Ali Banda areas that I grew up in,' ASR recalled.

After spending seven years in Warangal, where he completed his schooling and graduation, ASR returned to Hyderabad in 1983. The family then lived in the Santosh Nagar–Madannapet area.

Fissures in the Telugu State

The influence of the Andhra demographic had continued to grow through the 1980s and 1990s. In his prologue to the 2011 edition of Mir Laiq Ali's *Tragedy of Hyderabad*, statehood activist Dr Chiranjeevi Kolluri pulls no punches while describing the Andhra political class as neo-colonizers.[4]

As the Telugu Desam Party consolidated its power in the state, there was a sense that the Coastal Andhra elite was neglecting the Telangana region. The sectors where the disaffection was experienced acutely included education, real estate and irrigation projects. There was a cultural element to this disgruntlement: People from Telangana felt that the decision-makers and power brokers with roots in Coastal Andhra had a superiority complex.

The leftist activist Burgula Narsing Rao expressed this sentiment at a talk held at the Telangana Resources Centre in 2016. He identified the city's Jubilee Hills area as emblematic of the consumerist, ostentatious identity that was favoured by the Andhraites and which he felt had altered the soul of Hyderabad city. 'Jubilee Hills! Jubilee Hills!' Rao thundered, 'This five-star culture fabricated by the Andhra ruling classes glorified Jubilee Hills to such an extent that our youngsters are being destroyed by it.'[5]

There were other instances of this transformation. The gaudy, glitzy Chandana and Bommana Brothers shopping malls were more in vogue than homegrown enterprises such as Sultan Bazar's textile merchant Neelakantam Balakistaiah. Local eateries like Irani hotels were being supplanted by restaurants serving Andhra cuisine. The Telangana region and its people were heavily under-represented in the movies produced by the Telugu film industry, which had shifted base from Chennai to Hyderabad.

ASR's own professional shift came in this wider season of foment. Initially, he started preparing for the Civil Services while he pursued his PhD at OU's zoology department. But his heart was not in the world of science. He was initially attracted to journalism because he felt it would help along his exam preparation.

The present-day *Hindustan Times* correspondent for Telangana and Andhra Pradesh elaborated, 'I thought journalism would help me gain general awareness, which is very essential for the Civils. I got my first break in the industry at *News Time*, an English daily that was a part of the Eenadu Group. Then I got hired as a senior reporter at *Deccan Chronicle*, where I worked for nine years before moving to *Andhra Pradesh Times*.' After two years at *Andhra Pradesh Times*, in 1997, he rejoined *Deccan Chronicle* as a special correspondent. During that period, the Andhra–Telangana divide had riven newsrooms too.

ASR shared his memory of an instance when a colleague from Coastal Andhra claimed that the people of Telangana only began eating rice after NTR introduced a scheme to distribute the grain at Rs 2 per kilo. 'This individual thought we survived on just millets and coarse grains otherwise,' laughed ASR.

ASR also took umbrage at the lack of representation of the Telangana region in Telugu cinema. This sentiment, which was shared by many Telanganites, was expressed by the journalist Vayuvegula Subrahmanyam in his book *Telangana: Times of Turbulence, Triumph*. Subrahmanyam wrote,

> The point is, for Tollywood, Telangana simply does not exist. They could not see beyond the coastal and ceded regions. There could be a couple of films more but they were mostly about landlords and the exploitation of peasants and farm hands and the Naxalite movement when it shifted from Srikakulam to Telangana region. But the narrative had a heavy Andhra accent.[6]

When the region was represented, it was through characters who were either villains or secondary roles that provided comic relief.[7] A major marker that would identify them as Telanganite characters would be their heavily caricaturized Urdu-influenced dialect.

A Dormant but Real Sentiment

The first statehood struggle had died down in the early 1970s after Chenna Reddy struck a deal with Indira Gandhi.

Many students, especially those from OU, who had raised the banner for a separate Telangana went underground and veered towards Naxalism. Andhra domination intensified after the Telugu Desam Party (TDP), essentially a Coastal Andhra faction, had emerged as a strong alternative to the Congress, whose stronghold was the Rayalaseema region.

In 2004, the Congress came back to power, with Y. Rajasekhara Reddy as chief minister. Three years before this, KCR broke away from the TDP to form the Telangana Rashtra Samithi, a political party whose primary plank was statehood for Telangana.

The slogan '*Jai Telangana!*' would once again reverberate in Hyderabad.

When ASR's second child, Sruthi Vibhavari, was born in 1999, the family shifted from the Santosh Nagar–Madannapet area to Vanastalipuram.

The cries for a bifurcated Andhra Pradesh would grow louder in the next few years. One instance of the finer distinctions between Andhraites and Telanganites is the annual nine-day long festival of Bathukamma to thank Goddess Parvati for the year's crop harvest around September or October. ASR told me that Bathukamma was made fun of by people from Andhra. 'For a long time, my mother and the rest of my family never celebrated it outside our house. We used to do it indoors,' Sruthi explained, 'Only during summers in Warangal did I see our customs on display. The Telangana movement changed this and began bringing those manifestations out in the open.'

Marching for a State

On 28 November 2009, the Congress-led UPA Government in Delhi probably had a flashback to that fateful day when Potti Sriramulu's death sparked riots in Vizianagaram, Vishakapatnam, Vijayawada and other cities in the Madras Presidency's Telugu-speaking parts.[8]

Ever since the statehood movement received a fillip in 2009, bandhs and protests become commonplace. On 29 November that year, KCR had been arrested near Karimnagar when he began a fast unto death.[9] The very same day, Kasoju Srikanth Chary, a student in his twenties, set himself on fire.[10] Though KCR broke that fast eleven days later when the UPA government commenced the process to form a new state,[11] many such instances were to follow. Two months later, a nineteen-year-old student, S. Yadaiah, set himself on fire right outside the OU gate.[12]

ASR and his family were in favour of the new state. 'We felt Telangana possesses its own distinct culture when it comes to lifestyle, linguistic and culinary attributes,' ASR explained. His wife, Anitha, a teacher and school administrator, had been overlooked many times for promotions and other opportunities for professional advancement.

Though not as direct participants, ASR and his brother Apparasu Krishna Rao were supporters of the Telangana movement. Krishna Rao is currently an associate editor in the Delhi bureau of the Telugu newspaper *Andhra Jyothi*. He lobbied for the cause by submitting representations to the Justice Sri Krishna Committee, which had been set up in 2010 to examine the demand for statehood.

A year before that committee was formed, the Telangana Joint Action Committee (JAC) had been established to bring together political parties, organizations and other pro-statehood groups on a common platform.

The Million March protest, held on 10 March 2011, prompted the central government to take the demands for statehood seriously. Thousands of people marched towards the Tankbund area of the city. They raised pro-Telangana slogans, sang anthems demanding statehood and destroyed statues of Andhra icons that had been erected by the TDP establishment.

Anitha, ASR's wife, did not walk in the Million March, but she participated in the Sakkala Janula Samme that took place a few months later. Organized mainly by Professor Kodandram, who was on the Telangana JAC, this protest saw the involvement of teachers and students of both government and private colleges, road transport employee unions, schoolteachers and lawyers. Many others from the government sector went on strike for more than forty days.

Initially, ASR's daughter, Sruthi, simply enjoyed the holidays that were declared due to these shutdowns. But the true magnitude of the movement dawned on her when her mother participated in Sakkala Janula Samme.

'Subh-e-Azadi': The Morning of Freedom

Sruthi was fifteen in 2014, when the state of Telangana was finally born. She was not yet old enough to enjoy the culmination of the movement, but she remembers the moment when the first session of the Legislative Assembly convened. 'This is a house full of Telangana people only,' she told her father.

The one thing Sruthi liked about the first Telangana chief minister, KCR, was that he spoke in a dialect that many Telanganites call their own.[13] In 2017, her mother finally got her overdue promotion as school principal.

Urdu was made the state's second language and the Telugu film industry began to feel more representative of the region and its people. There was a spate of films where Telangana Telugu and Dakhani Urdu were presented on their terms, and not as caricatures. A good example of this kind of film was *Mallesham*, which was released in 2019. It tells the story of a rural everyman who faced numerous obstacles before inventing a machine that decreased the Pochampally weavers' manual effort from six hours to ninety minutes. In one scene, the titular protagonist is shown speaking Telangana Telugu, while Abdul, a minor character, responds in Dakhani.

'*Jambiya*', a song in the film, captured the composite culture of Telangana that comes alive during the Peerla Pandaga festival. It features the vocals of folk singer and poet Goretti Venkanna. Peerla Pandaga takes place in the month of Muharram, with both Hindu and Muslim villagers bearing alams (flagpoles topped with metal finials) and dancing around a fire pit to commemorate the martyrdom of Imam Hussain.

Yet, all has hardly been well in Telangana. In the past, KCR has been accused of bringing back a Nizam-like feudal state, where his kith and kin—namely those from his landed castes of which he is a part of—call the shots.[14]

For ASR and many Telanganites, the cultural revival in Telangana in the past decade was very welcome. However, he clarified, 'The state still has a long way to go in terms of providing excellent governance, rooting out corruption and bettering the common man's life.'

Channelling Makhdoom Today

As Sruthi grew older, she was able to contextualize the political and cultural significance of statehood. She currently works as a research analyst at an advisory firm for economic development. Now, she worries about the selective appropriation of the statehood struggle by communal elements that had not contributed to the movement in the first place.

The BJP might have been the among the first to formally advocate for bifurcation in 1997.[15] KCR may have taken up the cause years later but his shrewd maneouvres and oratory skills on the ground made all the difference in bringing Telangana into reality.[16] Plus, throughout the late 1990s and early 2000s, both the BJP and Congress dithered between granting statehood and strategically remaining silent on the issue.[17,18]

But the appropriation is just one small part of a larger trend that was apparent during the Greater Hyderabad Municipal Corporation (GHMC) elections in December 2020. The BJP's rhetoric in the run-up to the polls was communally tinged. Bandi Sanjay Kumar, then the state chief, promised to carry out a 'surgical strike' in the Old City to root out Rohingya refugees.[19] National leaders of the party, too, jumped onto the bandwagon—Home Minister Amit Shah claimed that the Majlis Ittehad-ul-Muslimeen and the TRS had failed to make Hyderabad a global city. Shah attributed this failure to the city's 'Nizam culture'.[20]

The vitriol continued long after the GMHC elections with Bandi Sanjay Kumar's open threat. 'We will definitely provoke communal hatred if the TRS continues to woo a community that constitutes a 12 per cent of the electorate,' he warned in the middle of 2021.[21]

Sruthi was concerned by all the rabble-rousing that has increasingly become a feature of public life in Telangana. 'As a society we have grown accustomed to the idea of corruption pervading governance and other aspects of life. But religious bigotry is something I can never accept,' she denounced.

Her words brought to mind a couple of lines from 'Baaghi', a poem by one of her grandfather's literary and political idols, Makhdoom Moinuddin.

Taffariqa-e-mazhab-o-millat ke mitaane de mujhe
Khwaab-e-farda ko bas ab haal banaane de mujhe[22]

Let me obliterate the discords of religion and communities
For I will also bring to existence in the present the dreams
of tomorrow

Raj Bahadur Gour: The Good Doctor

مساوات کے دیپ گھر گھر جلیں گے

سب اہلِ وطن سر اُٹھا کر چلیں گے

— حبیب جالب

Masaavaat ke deep ghar ghar jalenge
Sab ehl-e-watan sar utha kar chalenge

In every household shall the candle of equality shine bright
All my countrymen will hold their heads up high in plain sight

—Habib Jalib

Back to Road Number 12

In an apartment complex on Banjara Hills' famed Road Number 12 lives Oudesh Rani Bawa, a reservoir of knowledge about Hyderabad's history and Urdu literature. Born in 1940, she has witnessed the city's transformation from a princely centre of power to one of India's information technology capitals. Her late husband Dr Vasant

Kumar Bawa, an IAS officer and founder of the Centre for Deccan Studies, made significant contributions to scholarship on the Deccan. A biography on the seventh Nizam is one of the many books that he authored.

Whether I drop by just to say hello or to interview her for an article, I never fail to learn something new about Deccani history. When I went to see her in late 2022, our conversation did not revolve around Hyderabad's prolific Urdu poets or writers, as it does usually.

Instead, we spoke about her cousin Raj Bahadur Gour.

Gour, whom she referred to as 'Rajan Bhaiya', wore many hats over his long and enriching life. They include medical student, trade unionist, a rebel on the run, a Rajya Sabha member of Parliament and promoter of Urdu.

Many of the city's older litterateurs and leftists still smile at the mention of Gour's name. They remember his wit and the endearing way with which he used to speak and write. Whether it was to express the plight of an exploited worker or to poke good-natured fun at a comrade, Gour always had an Urdu or Persian couplet up his sleeve.

City historian Sajjad Shahid grew up interacting with Gour, as his parents had been friends with him since their Osmania University days before Police Action. Shahid once told me that speaking to Oudesh Rani Bawa is the closest thing to getting a taste of Gour's personality today. Rani Bawa is among the last few living people with a memory of the formative and later years of her cousin's life. Tamara, Gour's daughter, who was visiting from San Francisco, also joined us later on that December afternoon.

Gour was thirty at the time of Police Action. As a young man, he had lived through the hectic last decades of the Asaf Jahi's dynasty rule, over which the shadow of the British had loomed. Despite this setup, the kingdom was not impervious to the movements brewing beyond its borders. Rip-tides of the Indian National Congress' independence campaign and the fervour that brought about the

Bolshevik Revolution in Czarist Russia would rock the foundations of princely Hyderabad.

Students at OU had their eyes peeled and ears cocked up for what was afoot beyond the borders of Hyderabad and British India. When studying at OU, Gour first veered towards the Hyderabad State Congress. But when Gandhi called off the non-violent political resistance in Hyderabad, which was also called the satyagraha, he, like many young people then, concluded that it would take a communist revolution to topple Hyderabad's oppressive feudal structures.

Many of Hyderabad's dynamic young leftists came from urban, affluent households. Gour belonged to one such Kayastha family.

Kayasthas of Hyderabad

Kayasthas have traditionally been a writing caste, who have fulfilled the function of record-keepers and bureaucrats.[1] They were adept at picking up the languages of the ruling class in the places they found themselves. During Mughal rule, for instance, they had to master written and spoken Persian. They were often the interlocutors between the Muslim rulers and their Hindu subjects.[2] Considering their penchant for language, Kayasthas have left their mark on Persian, Urdu and Hindi literature.

In the early 1700s, the first Nizam brought many Kayasthas and Brahmo-Khatris with him as he broke away from a weakened Mughal Empire and consolidated his own dominion down south. Since then, Kayasthas have been a key part of every subsequent Nizam's administration.

A Learned Household

Raj Gour was born on 21 July 1918 in a well-connected family in the Old City's Gowlipura area. His grandfather, Hari Pershad Gour, was brought to Hyderabad from his native city Gosaijung, which is in present-day Uttar Pradesh, by Hyderabadi Kayastha Rai Jaswant Rai as a groom for his niece, Jhanjan Bibi. Pershad's two younger brothers—Rai Badri Pershad and Rai Jamuna Pershad—and a sister named Gomti Bai also accompanied him down south in the late 1800s.

When he came to Hyderabad, Hari Pershad began working for Ghalib-ul-Mulk Jung, an aristocrat of the Paigah nobility, the highest-ranking nobles in Hyderabad. In terms of hierarchy, the Paigah family was seen as second only to the Asaf Jahs. Pershad was made the Serrishtedar-e-Arab, the chief accountant to manage the expenses of the Arab soldiers in Jung's private army.

Gour was born to Pershad's elder son, Rai Mehboob Rai. But it was Pershad's other son, Rai Mehboob Narayan, who was a father figure to Gour. After the death of Raj's biological mother, Amravati, Mehboob Rai had married a woman from the Saxena sub-caste. He then went to live with his new in-laws since unions outside the biradari (sub-caste) were frowned upon back then. In his early years, Gour was looked after by his grandaunt, Gomti Bai.

'My father and Rajan Bhaiyya were very close,' Rani Bawa said. Mehboob Narayan and his nephew shared many interests. They both found solace in flipping through pages of books and the words buried between them. Reading and literary pursuits were often a family tradition in Kayastha families. 'Education was a given among Kayasthas,' Rani Bawa told me, 'Even in small households, intellectual discussions and mushairas were common. I was lucky to be a part of such gatherings during my childhood.'

From an early age, Gour had a flair for languages. His teachers Zulfiqar Ali Khan and Vamana Rao helped encourage his interest in English, and Tasadduq Hussain Jaisi, originally from Uttar Pradesh, ingrained in him a love for Urdu.[3] Mehboob Narayan had introduced him to Munshi Premchand's short stories and novels. These contributed to shaping his worldview and got him to think deeply about the experiences of the working class.

As an adolescent, Gour had already started reading books that introduced him to the radical values that brought about a revolution in imperial Russia. It was only a matter of time before he came under the influences of both the Congress and communist strands of the anti-feudal establishment struggle.

Clarion Calls in 1930s' and 1940s' Hyderabad

In 1929, Gandhi had visited the Vivek Vardhini High School in the Jam Bagh area of the city. The Mahatma's visit had galvanized the nationalist feelings in Hyderabad and brought to the fore some of the growing discontent against the establishment.[4]

The princely state was constantly being buffeted by the winds of change blowing at its edges. The Government of India Act of 1935 created provincial councils in British India. These provided legislative representation to Indians. The elections had brought the Indian National Congress to power in the provinces that surrounded Hyderabad. These provinces shared languages with some of the tracts of Nizam-ruled Hyderabad: Marathi, Kannada, Telugu. At the time, there were many rumbles taking place internally as well. The Andhra Mahasabha had become very active as its functionaries were going around the princely state's Telugu-speaking districts, teaching peasants about their rights.

One of the first shows of openly nationalist defiance came in Aurangabad in 1938, where students at an intermediate college sang 'Vande Mataram' instead of 'God Save the King', a song in praise of the Nizam.[5]

At the time, Raj Gour was on the verge of completing his intermediate studies in biology, physics and chemistry at OU. In the same year that the song began making waves in Aurangabad, Raj and some other students also began singing it in OU as well, thereby flagging off the movement in Hyderabad city.

The shadow committee of the Hyderabad State Congress (HSC) used to often meet at his house. When Raj joined Osmania Medical College, he found himself veering towards the Arya Samaj, which provided many recruits for the Congress.

On the personal front, Raj and his extended family travelled to their ancestral land between 1939 and 1940, where he got married a girl from Azamgarh district. His wife, Sanjogta, was the sister of Banarasi Das Bedhab, the well-known Hindi humour poet. She would give birth to two boys in the coming years. Unfortunately, both children would die before they turned ten.

In 1942, the Congress launched the Quit India movement. When Raj graduated in 1943, he thought of officially joining the satyagraha. But that year, the HSC withdrew the civil resistance upon Gandhi's insistence. This left Gour and his fiery colleagues disillusioned.

Gour even wrote to Akhtar Hassan's left-leaning newspaper, *Payaam*, to underscore how non-violent methods would fall short of helping India secure her freedom.

OU Comrades' Association

At OU, Raj and other pupils had been exposed to communist thought through professors like Habib-ur-Rahman, who had been a protégé of Marxist theorist Harold Laski in London.

In 1939, when Raj still identified with the Congress' ideology, some students had formed the OU Comrades' Association. Makhdoom Mohiuddin, a former OU student and charismatic poet, had been inculcating leftist ideals into students as an Urdu lecturer in City College. Membership of the Comrades' Association was gradually expanded to include students and educators from other colleges in Hyderabad.

Raj was heavily involved with campus activism. In 1941, as the vice president of the Osmania Medical College Students' Union and editor of the campus magazine, he raised his voice against low wages for medical graduates.[6] He was failed by a professor for this.

Raj even considered quitting his medical education midway to concentrate on writing and unionizing full-time. But his father pushed him to finish his medical degree. To ensure that he did so, Rai Mehboob Rai even met P.C. Joshi, the secretary of the Communist Party of India, in Bombay with a request: that he persuade Raj to finish his medical degree.[7]

Joshi convinced Raj to complete his education. But medicine was not his true calling. Instead, after finishing his degree, he threw himself into union work and activism in both Hyderabad city and rural Telangana.

Urban Hyderabad: A Hotbed of Exploitation

Nizam-era Hyderabad was India's richest princely state. Osman Ali Khan, the seventh Nizam, had commissioned and completed grand projects like the Osmansagar and Himayatsagar reservoirs. But this was also a kingdom that had been built on back-breaking and exploitative labour. In the city, the factory workers and labourers were exploited by the elite and the wealthy. In the button factories of Old City, for instance, workers—many of whom were women and children—worked for seven days a week, without sick leave and in deplorable conditions. In the Nizam's far-flung districts, tyrannical landlords kept landless peasants and farmers under their thumb.

The Majlis Ittehad-ul-Muslimeen believed that Muslim labourers who toiled in textile and button factories would support Asaf Jahi rule solely because of their religious connection. That too, despite their poor economic circumstances. Makhdoom did not think so.[8] He referred to the Muslim child labourers of the Deccan Button factory as 'our princes'.[9]

Makhdoom's poetry and words of encouragement helped workers understand that they need not resign themselves to their fates. He travelled extensively around the Nizam's dominions delivering fiery speeches. At one gathering in Sultan Bazar in 1943, while holding forth on the need for a representative government, Makhdoom thundered that Governor General Lord Linlithgow could not lead the country to war by simply 'wagging his tail'.[10] For this, he was arrested and slapped with a sedition charge. The matter even went to trial in a Hyderabad court.

The threat of arrest also loomed over Raj, as he rallied textile workers in Nanded, Gulbarga and Warangal. In 1946, there came a turning point in the peasants' uprising.

The Telangana Rebellion and the Ban on Communists

On 4 July 1946, a guerrilla leader Doddi Komarrayya was killed by landlord Ramachandra Reddy's goons. This killing removed the fear of police and Razakars among the districts' denizens.[11] Thousands of people stopped farming and took up arms.[12] As a result, the government's ability to collect grains and other taxes was severely affected.[13] The Telangana Peasants' Rebellion was now a full-fledged armed conflict.

Back in the city, relations between unions and industry magnates were deteriorating further. The All-India Trade Union Congress (AITUC), CPI's trade federation, was making its presence felt in Hyderabad. In October 1946, the Nizam's administration banned the CPI. As a result, anybody who had directly associated themselves with the CPI was under threat of incarceration. Arrest warrants were issued for Makhdoom Mohiuddin, Raj Bahadur Gour and Jawad Razvi.

Around this time, comrades in Hyderabad received a covert instruction from P.C. Joshi of the Central Committee.[14]

'Glue to earth,' the message said. It was a euphemism for going underground.

The Great Escape

Raj went on the run. Rani Bawa recalled a time when K.L. Kapoor, deputy superintendent of police, who also happened to be a friend of her father, came to her house in Gowlipura during Diwali. He was looking for Raj.

He asked to come in and check if Raj was there. The feisty Oudesh then answered, 'Chacha, you cannot come in. There are ladies inside.'

Those 'ladies' for whom it would be unsavoury for Kapoor to see also included communist leaders like Baddam Yalla Reddy and Ravi Narayan Reddy. Kapoor then protested that nothing would happen and that he was going to enter. Oudesh warned, '*Nahin aana aap!* (Do not come in!)'

Kapoor then slapped her only to have her hit him back and tear his kurta. Kapoor left. Oudesh went back into her house crying, 'Kishan Chacha hit me.'

In his book titled *Random Writings*, Gour wrote that the underground life was 'unknown' to him and several of his comrades. They were figuring it out as they went along. At night, they would move about freely, meeting party units and working committees of the unions.[15] It was not long before their game was up. In November 1946, Razvi and Gour were arrested at a left-leaning lecturer Akthar Hassan's house on the OU campus.

They were locked up in Hyderabad Central Jail for about five months. In May 1947, Raj was a free man again after an audacious prison break. The plan had been masterminded by K.L. Mahendra, a Shantiniketan graduate who had participated in union activities up in Bengal. He had enlisted the help of student activists Rafi Ahmed and Abdul Basith to execute the plan.

The state's security apparatus was occupied with a public meeting addressed by Jayaprakash Narayan at Secunderabad's Karbala Maidan. Meanwhile, Raj and Jawad had received word through a courier that they must feign a toothache. The jailer then transported them to the hospital for a check-up.

In Rani Bawa's telling, the prisoners were not made to wear handcuffs—only loose ropes were tied around the wrists. They were brought to the hospital where Raj Malliah, a medical union worker, took them to dental surgeon Dr Tajammul Hussain. Hussain was also in on the plan. Another OU medical student, Dr Paranjpe, a classmate of Raj's, ensured that no misgivings could put a spanner in the works. As they were taken to the front of the long line outside Dr Tajammul's office, a few patients caused a ruckus as to why the two prisoners were allowed to cut the line. Some policemen who were supposed to accompany Raj and Jawad showed up. But little did these policemen know that these people who were getting belligerent outside Hussain's office were not actually seeking dental care. They were actually comrades Rafi, Agamaiah and others who were posing as patients so that Raj and Jawad could make an escape.[16]

Raj and Jawad then walked out of the dental department from the back entrance and snuck into the adjacent mortuary. The exit to that mortuary lead to a street in Begum Bazaar. Comrade Basith was waiting outside for them in the getaway car.

On the Run During the Armed Struggle

After the escape, K.L. Mahendra had instructed Raj to join other comrades in the districts where the conflict was getting more intense. He was to go to Yadgir in the Kannada-speaking districts. Makhdoom would be arriving there while en route to Sholapur in the Marathi-speaking districts. In Yadgir, Raj was instructed to present himself at the house of Malappa Kollur, a Congressman with a leftist orientation.[17]

When Raj reached the area, he found that Malappa had already been arrested the night before and there was a police presence in his house. He escaped from the house and reached the railway station, where Makhdoom was waiting for him. Makhdoom instructed him to go back to Sholapur. Raj continued on to Guntakal, where Comrade Chari was to smuggle him into Guntur, a town in the neighbouring province of the Madras Presidency.[18]

He then made his way to Vijaywada. From there he infiltrated back into the Hyderabad state's Warangal district, which bordered the Madras Presidency.[19] As Raj went about carrying messages between party members within and outside Hyderabad, the arrests of communist forces and sympathizers were continuing unabated.

Gour then went to the CPI headquarters in Bombay to explain what was happening on the ground. In Pune, he met Govind Das Shroff and Baba Saheb Paranjpe, both of whom were Congressmen from Hyderabad's Marathi-speaking districts. He also addressed a public meeting under another name in Ahmednagar.[20]

In the midst of such adventurism, Raj tied the knot a second time with Brij Rani Gour, a comrade whom he had known since 1943.[21]

But just a few months after the nuptials, the Nizam and his government would be yesterday's news. In September 1948, the military action by India led to the incorporation of the princely state into the newly independent union. Having dispatched with the Asaf Jahs, the Indian Army had set its sights on communists. However, plenty more running and eluding was in store for Raj.

Surkh Sitara

Ibrahim Jalees's memoir *Do Mulk Ek Kahani* narrates a compelling anecdote from Raj Gour's underground days. Jalees was a writer and brother of *Siasat* co-founder Mehboob Hussain Jigar (Chapter 1). Sometime in the 1940s, he had switched allegiances from the progressive camp to Qasim Razvi's faction, which was clamouring for Hyderabad's independence.

In *Do Mulk Ek Kahani*, Raj is the titular 'Red Star' of the chapter 'Surkh Sitara'. With the Indian Army hot on his trail, Jalees is hiding out in a secluded location. He then hears a knock on the door. The man knocking is his old comrade Raj Bahadur Gour, whom he has not met in a year. Raj tells Jalees that he was with Makhdoom in the fields of Telangana, where 13,000 villagers had 'emerged as free human beings with the hammer and sickle guiding the way'.

The catch-up session is a friendly one, but the atmosphere is still tense and there is an elephant in the room. Jalees finally asks Raj if he has come to take revenge on him for abandoning the progressives and joining the Razakars. At this point, Raj reveals he has a pistol in his pocket. Even as the colour drains out of his friend's face, Raj says:

> Why, Mr Mujahid-e-Azam (great warrior)? Got you, didn't I? After inciting ordinary Muslims with your communalism and then driving them towards martyrdom, why shy away from the same path yourself? You should be ashamed, my friend! Exhorting underprivileged humans to offer themselves in the way of a martyr's heaven behind the safety of a microphone is easy. But when Raj is sitting with a gun in front of you, what now of those fiery speeches? You swore that you would protect the gentry's Islam by fighting until the last drop of blood. If not the first drop of your blood, I'm here to shed the last one.[22]

Then, laughing, Raj pulls out a packet of cigarettes from his pocket. Jalees breathes a sigh of relief. But Raj does not spare him a piece of his mind, letting him know that he pities what he has become by throwing his lot in with the Razakars, because of his 'lust for money, booze and women.' Despite all this, Raj reassures that he is here to help Jalees escape the Indian authorities. Raj gives him a place and time to show up. And that sets in motion a series of events that helps Jalees make his way to Pakistan.

Discord and Surrender

At the time of his cinematic meeting with Jalees, Raj Gour was still a fugitive himself. The Indian state was in no mood to tolerate the communists holding sway in the villages of Telangana. The bitterness cut both ways. There was no love lost for the Indian Republic for Raj and some of his fellow comrades—like their leader B.T. Ranadive, they believed that independence was a sham and would only perpetuate the feudal inequities that the colonial and princely states had left behind.

The Andhra Provincial Committee, under Puchalapali Sundarayya, wanted to continue the fighting. They felt that the Police Action was a smokescreen. In reality, there had been a deal between the Nizam and the Congress to quell the peasant rebellion.

But there were other voices in the party calling for a truce. One of them was Ajoy Ghosh, who had become general secretary of the party in 1951. Gradually, Raj and others at various levels of the party cast their lot with a growing contingent that leaned towards calling off the armed struggle.

The dilemma had riven the party into factions. Consequently, the decision was left to the Russian Cominform. Ajoy Ghosh, S.A. Dange, Rajeshwar Rao and Makineni Basavapunnaiah went to Moscow to see Stalin. The Russian leader was in favour of dropping the armed struggle, seeing as how it was limited to just four to five districts within Hyderabad state. If the Nizam had been unable to procure quick access to a port, how would the guerrillas be able to receive supplies from Stalin?

Finally, the CPI opted to compete with the Congress on the electoral stage. The message to party members on the run was to turn themselves in and then work for the cause within the ambit of the Indian Constitution.

The End of the Line

Before and after Police Action, Raj's family had often borne the brunt of his dissenting ways.

After the communists relented and agreed to fight electorally, the Indian government's attitude towards them thawed somewhat.

The belligerence came to be accompanied by an acknowledgment (especially on the part of Nehru) that the Left had been effective in addressing the grievances of peasants.[23] The Andhra Mahasabha helped redistribute land and livestock, worked to end forced labour and succeeded in achieving fair wages in some agrarian tracts.[24] The Hyderabad State Congress advised Nehru to use the carrot of agrarian reform even as it brandished the stick of military operations.[25]

M.K. Vellodi, Hyderabad's first chief minister, replaced the non-Telugu-speaking brigadier who led the army's onslaught with Captain Nanjappa. He then covertly put the word out that those who turned themselves in would have their cases 'favourably considered'. As a result, Raj surrendered on 24 April 1951.

Rani Bawa told me how her cousin's humour had not abandoned him even when one of his comrades was killed in front of him by the police at Rajgir Lake. An officer who questioned Raj asked, 'Is your name Raj Bahadur Gour?' to which he responded, 'Yes, that is my name.'

The officer then asked if his father's name was Rai Mehboob Rai.

'I was three years old, and I did not get to confirm if that indeed was his name,' he shot back at the officer.

He also enquired, 'Are you a doctor?'

Rather than simply say yes, Gour replied, 'What exactly ails you? I am a doctor and can help you.'

The answer to that question about his father's name had the officer wondering if Raj was insane. In a document that Rani Bawa said she accessed from the police archives, the interrogating officer had written that he never came across such a humorous man who laughed even in the face of death.

Because the authorities did not have a picture of Raj Gour, they tasked a collector from Nalgonda to identify their humorous, eccentric prisoner. When he heard about his answers to the interrogator's questions, the collector knew that the man the authorities spoke of was none other than the colourful Raj Bahadur Gour. This collector wasted no time in publishing a pamphlet about Raj's arrest from a printing press that published a lot of CPI collateral. He went about distributing those pamphlets around various newspapers' offices in both Nalgonda and Hyderabad.

Back in Hyderabad, one informant named Sardar Singh came to Rani Bawa's house at 5 a.m. and told her family that Raj had been killed. Her family then mourned in silence. Though three hours later, Singh returned with some good news. The pamphlets distributed by the collector made their way to various publications. Through newspapers, word of Raj's whereabouts eventually reached the power corridors of Hyderabad state, but the authorities did not let Raj go easily. For three days, he was tortured in the Warangal camp. He was then transferred to Nalgonda jail.

While these proceedings were playing out, many leftists in Hyderabad were campaigning for state and national elections through the People's Democratic Front (PDF). From jail, Raj Gour had filed papers to contest for a Rajya Sabha Parliament seat during the 1951 election on a PDF ticket.

He won, but he was only let out of prison after Vice President Sarvepalli Radhakrishnan expressly requested for elected members to be physically present on the floor of the house and not in jail.[26]

Rani Bawa remembered the day of his release as if it were yesterday. There was a wedding to attend in the extended family. However, when her Rajan Bhaiya called and told her that he is coming, she hugged her father and declared, '*Mere ku Gowlipura jaane ka hai. Shaadi vaadi ki aisi ki taisi* (I want to go to Gowlipura. Forget the wedding).'

A Warrior for Urdu and Labourers

Gour's daughter Tamara, who was born while Raj was in hiding,[27] then joined Rani Bawa and me. Tracing the long and action-packed arc of Gour's life, we had reached the point where Tamara had a first-hand memory of moments and events. Although she was only a child when her father was in the Parliament, Tamara began talking about the way legislative debates were conducted. 'The criticism that parties and members levied upon each other was healthy, be it Congress leaders or anyone else,' Tamara said. 'There might have been differences on the floor, but the second everybody left the session, they would be cordial. My father had so much admiration for Jawaharlal Nehru.'

During his time in Parliament, Gour raised his voice for two causes that were dear to him—workers' rights and Urdu. He brought up the fact that workers in trade unions, who spoke little to no English, were unable to correspond with the labour department in their regional languages.[28] In 1958, he spoke out against the push for automation in the textile industry.[29]

Gour also called out the poor writing and language in *Aaj Kal*, an Urdu magazine edited by poet Josh Malihabadi and put out by the government's Publications Division.[30]

Oudesh told me that Josh rebuffed this with the following allegation. 'Raj Bahadur Gour is from the south. What does he know about Urdu? He just wants to shut the magazine down.' Even Jagan Nath Azad, who is considered to be the premier authority on poet Allama Iqbal, ended up presuming that Gour had malicious intentions. Sahir Ludhianvi then had to tell Josh that Gour was a true son of Urdu and had studied at a university where the language was the medium of instruction. Azad also came to realize that the Rajya Sabha MP's criticisms were not only constructive, but well-intentioned.[31]

That was not Raj's only criticism of the Publications Division. When an Urdu translation of a pamphlet on land reforms was up not to the mark, he took up the matter with G. Rajagopalan, the parliamentary secretary to the information and broadcasting minister.[32] The complaint was attended to by the minister, K.V. Keskar, who claimed that it was hard to find and train people for specialized translation work. Gour was incredulous. 'Do we not have people to translate a work on agriculture?' he asked.

After completing two terms in the Rajya Sabha, in 1962 he declined to contest a third time. Plus, he wanted younger blood to take his place there. His sights were now on state politics, where the communists were more than holding their own in the face of the electoral juggernaut that was the Congress.

Back to a Hyderabad in Flux

In the short-lived Hyderabad state of the early 1950s, the PDF communists were a powerful opposition to the Congress. In the 1951–52 assembly election, they garnered 39.59 per cent of the vote share, second only to the Congress's 42.32 per cent.[33] Their influence did not wane dramatically even after Hyderabad state's trifurcation. In the 1957 assembly polls of a unified Andhra Pradesh, the PDF won the second-highest vote share once again.[34] Five years later, Gour contested the Pathergatti assembly seat on a CPI ticket, only to lose to the MIM's Sultan Salahuddin Owaisi.[35]

The Left was also active in Hyderabad's cultural and artistic scene, which was regaining its vibrancy in the aftermath of Police Action, the peasants' rebellion and states' reorganization. Times of great social and political churn are known to inspire art that is sensitive and detail-oriented.

Artists' guilds associated with the PDF and the CPI organized programmes around music and humorous poetry to help the public regain its verve and to re-establish solidarity between Hindus and Muslims. Raj Bahadur Gour, by virtue of this position as City Party Secretary and member of the Andhra Pradesh Executive Committee, was at the forefront of these efforts.

One of the hubs for such activities was the Bachelors' Quarters building besides the Moazam Jahi Market. The building became a meeting point for those straddling the worlds of leftist politics and artistic endeavour.[36] It was a site of campaigning and trade union activity that Raj carried out. Tamara told me that she had seen stalwarts like ghazal maestro Vithal Rao, painter Saadat Ali Khan, singer Mumtaz and music composer Iqbal Qureshi in the building. 'I was so fortunate to have been around such talent growing up,' Tamara said. 'The artists' egos were not as inflated back when I used to go. I even performed in the Qadir Ali Baig-directed play, *Darwaze Khol Do*, which Krishan Chander wrote.'

Doing Justice to Maulana Azad

Being of the CPI mould that had stood firm on its demand for a Vishalandhra or a unified Telugu state, Gour had nothing to do with the 1969 agitation for Telangana's statehood. He had long believed that the migration of the Andhra population from the Madras Presidency would diffuse and dissolve the bitter legacy of Police Action and the Armed Rebellion. Despite that, 1969 turned out to be a landmark year for Gour. The untimely death of Makhdoom Mohiuddin in August that year was no less than a family tragedy. The poet known as Shayar-e-Inquilaab died after a sudden heart attack in Delhi, where he was attending a national council meeting of the AITUC.

Tamara left to study in Moscow in 1970. Eight years later, her father made one last attempt at running for public office. He contested for a Lok Sabha seat from the Secunderabad constituency, but he came up short in his bid.

From that point, he turned more of his attention to Urdu activism. He was heavily involved in fundraising for Urdu Hall, a cultural space for Urdu literary events and an evening college. By 1980, he started relinquishing all party posts.

His physical health had begun to deteriorate by 1990. He had the same fervour for ground-level activity but it had become increasingly difficult for him to spend a lot of time outdoors. During this time, he wrote several opinion pieces in newspapers like *Siasat* and *Munsif*. *Adbi Jaaiza* and *Adbi Tanazur*, both works of literary criticism, were also published in 1991.

As a member of the I.K. Gujral-led Committee for the Promotion of Urdu, he also played his part in ensuring that Hyderabad would become the home of a higher learning institution that inherited the legacy of his alma mater.

When Indrajit Gupta served as Union Home Minister during the mid-1990s, the committee convened to discuss the location and name of a new Urdu-medium university. Several members and politicians suggested New Delhi or Lucknow.[37] However, Raj Gour made sure that this proposed university would be built in his hometown.

Some had proposed that the university be named after Indira Gandhi. Raj asserted that there was no one more deserving of the honour than Maulana Abul Kalam Azad. Tamara told me that her father strongly believed that India's first education minister did not get his due in the national imagination. She stressed, 'He felt that justice had not been done to Azad, who had remained a hardcore nationalist, no matter what.'

Preserving Family History

When the Telangana statehood struggle was gaining stream in the late 2000s, Raj was at the tail end of his life.

Talking about the period when KCR raised his pitch for a new state, Tamara mentioned, 'The chaos that ensued in the late 2000s really affected him. He was very *aman-pasand* (peace-loving).' Raj had always felt that the Telugu-speaking territories would develop better if both the Andhra and Telangana regions worked together, especially since the former had plenty of financial capital and the latter was low on natural resources. Raj did not live to see the bifurcation. He breathed his last on 7 October 2011.

We had finally reached the end of the remarkable life story of Raj Bahadur Gour. Tamara excused herself for a few minutes. When she came back, she handed me a booklet. The front page read, *Nana: An Interview of Dr. Raj Bahadur Gour By Master Praveen Balaji.*

As an eleven-year-old, Tamara's son, Praveen, had chronicled his grandfather's trajectory. When I read it a day later, I found it to be a fascinating oral account of the first five decades of Raj Gour's life.

Praveen, now a software engineer, and his brother, Pavan, a computer scientist, currently live in the Bay Area of California. Like Vasiq Sarwari (Chapter 4), they were a part of the wave of engineering graduates who left India for the USA in the 1980s and 1990s.

One More Pearl of History from Road Number 12

Despite spending most of her time in the US, Tamara Gour visits the city often. She then began talking about Mah Laqa Bai Chanda, the renowned, influential figure in the courts of the second and third Nizams. Rani Bawa then told me that back in 2013, she wrote a monodrama about this unique woman who held some sway in the Asaf Jahi dispensation. Prominent actor and theatre figure of Hyderabad Vinay Varma directed this opus that was staged at three different venues. One was the historical Taramati Baradari, a pavilion built by the fourth Qutub Shahi ruler for his favourite courtesan. The others were the famed Ravindra Bharati Auditorium and the happening cultural space that is Lamakaan.

As she elaborated on the history of Mah Laqa Bai Chanda, the faint hum of recognition in my head was progressively getting louder. That is when it struck me that I had read about Mah Laqa Bai Chanda briefly in *Tazkira-e-Darbar-e-Hyderabad*, a history of Asaf Jahi Hyderabad authored by Raman Raj Saxena, one of Rani Bawa's uncles.

Yet another saga of Hyderabad's history had neatly folded over itself, criss-crossing generations and, despite all odds, surviving to the present.

Narayan Raj Saxena: A Saga of Poets and Patriots

یہ جبر بھی دیکھا ہے تاریخ کی نظروں نے

لمحوں نے خطا کی تھی صدیوں نے سزا پائی

— مظفر رزمی

Yeh jabr bhi dekha hai taareekh ki nazron ne
Lamhon ne khata ki thi, sadeeyon ne saza paayi

History has been a witness to this tragedy
The mistakes of moments have brought suffering to
mankind for centuries

—Muzaffar Razmi

Hyderabad Ke Bansi Raja

In November 2020, I put on an N95 mask and ventured to the Chowk
area—Hyderabad's hub for rare books in Old City, for the first time
since the pandemic. Haziq & Mohi, the store I went to, has been
a favourite of historians and writers such as William Dalrymple,[1]

the British author of *White Mughals*, and John Zubrzycki, the Australian author of The *Last Nizam*.[2] At Haziq & Mohi, treasures in English and Urdu find refuge on decrepit shelves and cluttered stacks. An Urdu book lying on a dusty heap caught my eye. Its cover featured an image of a royal-looking, immaculately dressed individual, with the Charminar in the background.

The title of the book was *Hyderabad Ke Bansi Raja* and its author was Dr Bhaskar Raj Saxena. The man in the image was the titular Bansi Raja, whose real name was Girdhari Pershad and whose pen name was 'Baaqi'. Bansi Raja was a trusted political aide of the sixth Nizam, Mahbub Ali Khan.

As I flipped through the pages, the name rang a bell. In the dog days of the summer, cooped up at home during the lockdown, I had read Karen Leonard's *Social History of an Indian Caste: The Kayasths of Hyderabad*. The book mentioned that the Saxena biradari (sub-caste) of Kayasthas had given the Deccan some of its most illustrious poets. One of them was Bansi Raja himself.

Leonard wrote that apart from being a prolific Urdu and Persian poet, Bansi Raja had introduced many Urdu poets from north India to the sixth Nizam Mahbub Ali Khan, a great patron of the arts.[3]

Now, looking at *Hyderabad Ke Bansi Raja*, I learnt that the author was a great-grandson of Baaqi. I ended up buying the paperback for Rs 1,600—sixteen times its price when it was first published in 1995.

Throwing Darts in the Dark

About a month later, in December 2020, I was at the Banjara Hills home of a Mathur-Kayastha family friend with whom my father went way back. By that time, I had already begun working on this book project. I told him that I was seeking information on Police Action and Urdu literature authored by Kayasthas. He connected me to Anoop Raj Saxena, whose house happened to be a stone's throw away from mine.

For the meeting with Anoop, I carried five books that were authored by his relatives. Two were rubaai (quatrain) collections by his uncle Dr Raghunandan Raj Saxena, who went by the pen name 'Ilhaam'. There were two books by Raman Raj Saxena: *Tazkira-e-Darbar-e-Hyderabad*, which chronicles the tenures of all seven Asaf Jahi monarchs; and *Aasma Jah Ka Hyderabad*, a detailed account of Paigah noble Aasma Jah's contributions as the prime minister. Of course, I also took with me *Hyderabad Ke Bansi Raja*.

The same photograph of Girdhari Pershad on the cover of the book hung on the wall of Anoop Raj Saxena's living room. I was not surprised to learn that the picture had been taken by the renowned state photographer Raja Deen Dayal. Bansi Raja is also from Anoop's family.

Seeing my interest in learning about the history of one of the great Kayastha families of Hyderabad, Anoop referred me to his cousin Narayan Raj, who was eighty-one years old, lived in Panjagutta and had more of a literary inclination.

Meeting Narayan Raj Saxena

Despite not being in the best of health, Narayan Raj agreed to meet me. In December 2020, we spoke in the living room of his Panjagutta residence, where I saw the same photograph of Bansi Raja on the wall again. Narayan Raj sat on the sofa in front of me, wearing an N95 mask. He needed the support of a walker to move around. After I introduced myself and the project, he started telling me about the Saxenas.

This first conversation was centred on the contribution of his family to the Urdu landscape. We exchanged the names of many wordsmiths and titles. As we were speaking, I suddenly remembered the book *Shahan-e-Asafiya aur Hindu Muslim Rawadari* (published in English as *The Religious Tolerance of Asaf Jahi Kings and Hindu-Muslim Traditions*) and mentioned it. The book, authored by Sheela Raj, had come in handy for a long feature that I had written for

The Hindu Business Line's features supplement on the seventieth anniversary of Police Action. I then asked, 'Do you know about Sheela Raj's book, and are you related to her?'

Narayan Raj perked up noticeably. 'Of course! She was my wife,' he answered.

It had been a couple of years since I had read *Shahan-e-Asifiya aur Hindu Muslim Rawadari*. In the previous month, I read *Hyderabad Ke Bansi Raja*. And here I was, sitting across Sheela Raj's husband and Dr Bhaskar Raj Saxena's brother.

Narayan Raj then said, warmly, '*Ap apna ich ghar samjho yeh. Mere khaandaan aur Police Action ke baare mein abhi guftagoo ho sakti ya ap kisi aur wakht pe bhi aa sakte sawaalon ka ehtimaam kar ke* (Think of this as your own home. We can speak in detail about my family and Police Action now or some other time after you prepare some questions).'

I told him that I would prepare and come another time. Before I left, Narayan Raj asked me to pick up his own book from the shelf. He said it contained a background of the family, and would help me prepare for our next interview. That is how I came into possession of a copy of Narayan Raj Saxena's *Saga of a Kayasth Family*.

An Illustrious Lineage

Saga of a Kayasth Family suggests that the family's roots go all the way back to the early 1700s, when a Kayastha official came to Hyderabad with the first Nizam, Qamaruddin Khan. Daulat Rai originally belonged to Chhibramau, in present-day Uttar Pradesh.

His son Raja Ram Pershad performed key administrative duties in the early days of the Asaf Jahi empire,[4] when Hyderabad state was still being fought over by the French, the British and the Mysore sultan. Swami Pershad, third in this line, had been the superintendent of the royal household during the reign of the third Nizam, Sikandar Jah.[5]

Rai Narhari Pershad then wore many hats for Sikandar Jah—manager of the armies that protected the royalty's private lands, supervisor of the royal kitchen, chief clerk and record-keeper.[6]

Bansi Raja, son of Rai Narhari Pershad, then became one of the most trusted, eminent officials in the royal court of the sixth Nizam.

In *Hyderabad Ke Bansi Raja*, the page just before an extensive family tree that spans two centuries, contains Girdhari Pershad's many titles.[7] Some designations include mentor to Mir Mahbub Ali Khan and the serrishtedar (chief accountant) of the Nizam's irregular and regular armed forces.

Dwarka Pershad Lucknowi's Persian couplet in the preface of the book indicates that modern titles of 'political aide', 'advisor' and 'right-hand man' may not do justice to the place that Bansi Raja occupied in the administration:

Khitaabash Bansi Raja az Nizam ast
Ba-wasf hameeda naik naam ast[8]

The Nizam bestowed this title of Bansi Raja
And by way of his approval of this title-holder's trustworthy qualities

Much before Mahbub Ali Khan had come to power, Girdhari Pershad had also been useful to Salar Jung I. Jung was a powerful Prime Minister who heralded in an age of administrative reform during the rule of the fourth Nizam, Nasir-ud-Daula.[9]

The Prime Minister had tapped Pershad to settle the salaries of soldiers in the army. Seeing the efficiency with which Pershad worked, a high-ranking noble named Raunaq Ali Khan Shah Yar-ud-Daula Shah Yar-ul-Mulk had asked him to manage his private army.[10]

Pershad's second son, Narsing Raj, held high posts in the banking and railways departments.[11]

Masters of the Verse

After familiarizing myself with these antecedents, I returned to Narayan Raj's residence in December 2020. With both his and his brother's books in front of me, I turned to page 169 of Narayan Raj's *Saga of a Kayasth Family* to point out a couplet I really liked. I began reading a verse from the chapter on that page.

> *Kyun bhatakta hai tu ay Saaqi kisi ke waaste*

> Why do you wander for anyone O' Saaqi

Before I could even complete the verse, Saxena recited the rest from memory.

> *Kaaba tere dil mein hain but-khana tere dil mein hai*

> The Kaaba is in your heart, the temple of idols is in your heart

These lines had been written by his father Narhar Raj who composed Urdu poetry under the pen name of 'Saaqi'. Narhar Raj's father Narsing Raj was also a poet who wrote under the pen name 'Aali'.

Being one of the sixth Nizam's trusted associates, Bansi Raja had access to Mirza Khan, a kind of poet laureate in Mahbub Ali Khan's court. The poet, better known as Daagh Dehlvi, had this to write on the death of Bansi Raja:

> *Baikunth ko jab sidhaare Raja naagaah*
> *Kya sadma-o-gham dil ko hua hai jaankah*
> *Likh Daagh yahi swargbaasi ka to*
> *Karta rahe baaqi aur faani ay aah*[12]

> When Raja suddenly left for the heavenly abode
> I wept and wallowed

Oh Daagh, through this tribute for the departed soul
May he remain immortal in this world of the ephemeral

Today, any Persian influence on Indian culture is seen as a forced implant from Central Asia. Persian is seen as a language that supplanted—and not supplemented—Sanskrit after north India came to be invaded and ruled by Muslim kings and dynasties. But Daagh's lines above challenge this assumption. His tribute to Bansi Raja is sprinkled with words from both Sanskrit and Persian.

A similar observation could be made about Bansi Raja's own poetry. Having the Kayastha flair of languages, he was also fluent in Hindi and Urdu. This felicity with languages is an inherited trait among the Saxenas. Narayan Raj told me about his father Narhar Raj's translation of the *Yog Vashisht*, a philosophical text. 'He translated it from Sanskrit to Hindi,' Narayan Raj said. 'He did this during the last fifteen years of his life, which he spent mostly in the Keshavgiri temple located in the Chandrayangutta area of Old City.'

Saga of a Kayasth Family contains a careful curation of works by family members, which were variously written in Hindi, Braj Bhasha and Urdu. In 1890, for instance, Bansi Raja had translated the *Shiv Puran* from Braj and Awadhi Bhasha into Urdu.[13] This text would be published in Devanagari script only in 2017.[14]

These linguistic abilities and learned temperaments were of value to the Asaf Jahi setup. Narhar Raj, Narayan Raj's father, had worked with the excise department of the seventh Nizam's administration.[15] Like some of his ancestors, he was then made the main supervisor of the gardens of the Asaf Jahi crown lands. Narhar Raj's career in the administration coincided with the beginning of the end of the princely state of Hyderabad. There was political tumult in the Nizam's dominions and it could be attributed to two causes: the inequity perpetuated by the Asaf Jahi establishment; and the nationalist movement that was gaining steam in the rest of the country.

Dispensers of Justice

Hyderabad was no longer immune to the winds of change that were blowing in British India. For one, the Arya Samaj, the Hindu reform-cum-revivalist organization founded by Dayanand Saraswati in 1875, had consolidated its presence in the Marathi-speaking districts of the Nizam's dominions sixteen years later.[16] Soon enough, the organization began making its presence felt in Hyderabad city.

In the early 1900s, under the leadership of Gaya Pershad, the Arya Samaj focused more on religious and social reform.[17] By the late 1920s, however, the Samaj's social activities took on a nationalistic tinge—its membership had taken on a different character.[18] In Hyderabad, the Samaj's political colour had become more overt. The leadership had passed on to those who openly challenged the Nizam's continued rule in the Deccan.

One of the key men in the Samaj was Pandit Narender ji, who belonged to a Saxena family from the Shah Ali Banda area of the Old City. A gifted orator, he travelled around Hyderabad state delivering fiery speeches that advanced the Samaj's brand of religious nationalism. 'Hindus! Rise and tear out the root of the tree of Hyderabad!'[19] was the kind of thing he said when he called for a boycott of Muslim merchants.

In the 1930s, the Samaj found a foil in the Majlis-Ittehad-ul-Muslimeen, which had been similarly founded with a social and religious agenda by Maulana Mahmood Nawaz Khan in 1927. But, like the Samaj, the MIM had turned political as independence came close.

The MIM's communal turn was spearheaded by Bahadur Yar Jung, a dynamic preacher who was elected as the organization's president in 1938. The Arya Samaj and the MIM had fanned the communal flame in Hyderabad, which had lived through a period of famed communal amity under the Nizam Mahbub Ali Khan.

It got to a point where the Nizam's administration barred both Pandit Narender ji and Jung from giving speeches. However, the two ideologues were undeterred.[20]

Narayan Raj was a child at the time. Given the family connection, he spent a lot of time around Pandit Narender ji. But the family also had a connection to Bahadur Yar Jung. Narsing Raj, Narayan Raj's grandfather, had once mediated a high-profile property dispute between Jung and his brother. 'Maharaja Kishen Pershad had offered to mediate,' Narayan Raj told me, referring to the Prime Minister of the sixth and seventh Nizam, 'But he had become busy with affairs of the state and had asked Narsing Raj to carry out the mediation.'

After Narsing Raj successfully resolved the dispute, the Kayastha community's estimation had risen in Jung's eyes. Narayan Raj told me an anecdote from the time when Muhammad Ali Jinnah, who was a close associate of Jung's, came to Hyderabad. Jung had introduced Narsing to Jinnah, while remarking, '*Insaaf inn logon se seekhna chahiye* (These people can teach us a lot about delivering justice).'

Dispute resolution and mediation was seen as a hereditary skill, with Kayasthas perfectly placed to play the impartial interlocutors in disputes between Muslims. Bansi Raja, too, had an exemplary record of resolving conflicts. And the disputes were many—squabbles within the royal and noble families were quite common, and so were disagreements between the Yemini-Arabs and Pashtun troops that served in the regular and irregular armies.[21]

The Mistakes of Moments

At the time, Narayan Raj was an elementary school student at Madrassa-e-Aliya. Along with the Arya Samaj and the MIM, the Congress and leftists had developed their own support base in Hyderabad. When I asked him about the political leanings of the Kayastha community at this time, Narayan Raj responded in broad terms. 'Kayasths are not people who involve themselves in conflicts of interest. In the Mughal era, they learned Persian and Urdu. That helped them earn jobs and high offices. Different degrees of adaptability to changing circumstances would be key to finding kinship among fellow human beings or even patronage from powerful entities.'

When I enquired as to whether history had been tough on Osman Ali Khan, he recited a couplet by Muzaffar Razmi:

> *Yeh jabr bhi dekha hai taareekh ki nazron ne*
> *Lamhon ne khata ki thi, sadeeyon ne saza paayi*

> History has been a witness to this tragedy
> That mistakes of moments have brought suffering to mankind for centuries

Narayan Raj then said, 'Had it not been for Police Action, my grandfather Narsing Raj would have been a minister in the Nizam's government. The portfolio was not decided but a farmaan (royal decree) had been issued for his appointment.'

The 'mistakes of moments' he referred to through the Razmi couplet was an allusion to the reign of terror that Qasim Razvi of the MIM had unleashed. 'Once Narsing Raj was invited to a jalsa (public gathering) at Purana Pul. Despite the fact that he was making a pro-Nizam speech, two Razakars had their swords drawn out and were watching him intently the whole time.'

Fearing for the safety of this family in that bloodthirsty and uncertain environment, Narsing Raj had shifted them to Bangalore for nine months. 'Osman Ali Pasha was actually a good human being,' Narayan told me, 'Why he did not crush Qasim Razvi with the snap of his fingers is just beyond me.'

Post-Police Action, Narayan Raj went to study at All Saints' School. He later completed his BSc and PhD in dairy sciences from Osmania University. After that, in 1971, he moved to Mumbai to work for Amul, the dairy cooperative.

A Disciple of a Long-Gone Mahbub Ali Khan

Narayan Raj Saxena married Sheela Raj, a renowned historian and writer. Before that, Sheela had been appointed as a lecturer in the Mahbubia Girls College.

Even after the couple moved to Mumbai, Sheela continued to work on aspects of Hyderabad's history. She was particularly fascinated by the reign of Mahbub Ali Khan, the sixth Nizam. In 1982, she channelled this interest into a PhD from Shreemati Nathibai Damodar Thackersay Women's University. The result of this endeavour was a thesis titled *The Socio-Economic and Cultural History of Hyderabad During the Reign of Nizam VI 1896–1911.*

The reign of the sixth Nizam is viewed as the golden period of Hyderabad. Some historians and many elite Muslim families consider the period as a time when the city reached its pinnacle as a prosperous melting pot of religions and cultures.[22] Its reputation as a centre for Urdu literature grew by leaps and bounds during this time. Poets like Daagh Dehlvi and Ameer Minai received patronage from Mahbub Ali Pasha, an aesthete who loved spending time with artists and musicians.

Narayan Raj told me his wife would respectfully refute anyone who spoke ill of Mahbub Ali Khan, his son Osman, or their descendants. After Sheela's passing in 2008, Narayan Raj would continue to publish her scholarly works through the Narhari Pershad Charitable Trust.

While handing me a copy of Sheela's thesis, he mentioned, 'This is an authoritative book, unlike the unsavoury and unsubstantial *The Days of the Beloved*.' This was not the first time that I had heard that this title—authored by Harriet Ronken Lynton and Mohini Rajan— was an unfair portrayal of Mahbub Ali Pasha. I had heard similar criticism from many who felt that the writers had relied on second-hand gossip more than archival research.

Sheela Raj was prolific in her lifetime. She had translated *Tosha-e-Aquibat*, Bansi Raja's travelogue of his spiritual journey across India, from Persian to Urdu. She also used to write well-informed columns about the heritage of India and Hyderabad in *Siasat*.

Towards the end of our conversation, I was keen to get his opinion on more contemporary times. As a gateway into this topic, I quoted an excerpt from the new chapter in the third edition of Karen Leonard's *Social History of an Indian Caste*, published in 2020. Leonard quoted an anonymous Mathur Kayastha youth as saying:

> Though the circumstances have changed since 1948, we have not woken up to the new reality. Living on the largesse of the Nizam for long …[we] imbibed a lot of cultural traits from the Nizam and ignored our native past … The new generation is now questioning that and changing its style … The Nizams and their Razakars have inflicted a lot of pain on the Hindus of Telangana … It is time to shed that legacy and move ahead.[23]

'This talk of a "native past" makes no sense,' Narayan Raj replied, 'Because never did the Nizams ask us to convert. We were able to write about our religions. Our families are strict followers of the Sanatan Dharma. We were Sanatan Dharmis then, and we are Sanatan Dharmis now.'

He noted that people should refer to the books written by him and his brother for information on how the Asaf Jahis patronized the construction of Hindu places of worship and the writing of religious texts.

In *Hyderabad Ke Bansi Raja*, there is a whole section devoted to the Keshavgiri temple in Chandrayangutta, which had been constructed during the Qutub Shahi era. After it was abandoned by priests and worshippers during the First War of Independence in 1857, the fifth Nizam had granted about 405,000 feet of land to encourage more settlement around the temple.[24] Viqar-ul-Umra, a prominent noble, also granted an extra 675,000 feet.[25]

'Viqar-ul-Umra used to celebrate Nag Panchami at his place and Asma Jah held Sankranti festivities in Basheer Bagh,' Narayan Raj continued, 'but today if you ask some Muslims to put on a little colour during Holi, it amounts to apostasy for them.'

An older Mathur's anonymous quote from the third edition of Leonard's book, puts Narayan Raj's assessment of current times into perspective. This individual took pride in the poetry, music and food of the Asaf Jahi era. At the same time, he highlighted certain current trends that he found disturbing.

> However, there is a divergence and polarization that has happened in the past twenty to thirty years, due to the rise of Right wing thought and politics on both the Hindu and Muslim sides and globalization ... There is more hard-line, conservative thinking due to the influence from the Middle East and specifically Saudi Arabia, where many Hyderabadi Muslims live, which we don't like at all. Like a significant portion of the educated Indian middle class, many Mathurs have become supporters of the RSS and BJP on the Hindu Right.[26]

This excerpt was from 2015. But when I spoke to Narayan Raj about this five years later, about these changes in society, by no means did he call for young people to learn Urdu and Persian, especially when English provided more socio-economic mobility. 'We have to respect the past without living in it though,' Narayan Raj advised.

That was not the last time I saw Narayan Raj Saxena. I ventured to his house three more times, twice before the second Covid-19 wave and once after that. When I went in early 2022 to say hello, his health had clearly worsened after his young brother's passing. I knew he did not have much time left. A few weeks later he died.

Another repository of history was gone.

However, one thing became clear from my conversations with Saxena, my own experiences with Kayastha family friends since 2013 and the third edition of Karen Leonard's book. The trajectories of some Hyderabadi Kayasthas blend seamlessly with the power structures of different eras.

But with respect to certain internal dynamics within the community, the sub-caste (biradari) groupings played a huge role in the Kayastha society of princely Hyderabad.

A Sense of Belonging

When it came to marriages, educational institutions, professional and political associations among Kayasthas in Asaf Jahi Hyderabad—the sub-caste mattered a lot. In the late 1800s, Brahmo-Khatris and Mathur Kayasthas opened their own school in Old City, where they imparted Western education.[27] The Mathurs and Srivastavas had their own associations as did the Saxenas of Hussaini Alam.[28] During the 1930s, a Mathur–Saxena marriage was seen as taboo.[29]

Partly due to the early efforts of Gaya Pershad and his mentor Kunwar Bahadur in the late 1800s, such rigidity among various sub-castes began to loosen.[30] Post-Police Action, exclusive organizations based on these groupings were far and few between, but in 1970, the Mathur Kayasthas formed the Hyderabad Mathur Kayasth Education and Welfare Society (HMKEWS).[31] The society leads entrepreneurship and education initiatives for their biradari members.

A few months after Narayan Raj's death, I spoke to a well-known Hyderabadi physician, Dr Ravi Karan, whose wife was related to Saxena. Born in 1944, he grew up in a Hyderabad that was rising from the ashes of Police Action.

Ravi, whose in-laws are Saxenas, had a defined view on the trajectory of the Kayastha community, from Police Action to the present-day. He is also a former HMKEWS president; he now serves as an advisor.

Be it in Karen Leonard's book or during our conversation, he made one observation clear: Kayasthas had not quite taken to Telugu.

'After 1948, it was hard to get a government job without knowing English. With Telugu, one could not do much back then. Nowadays, it helps for bureaucratic or political careers,' Ravi Karan said. 'For the past seventy-five years, Kayasthas have not imbibed Telugu with the alacrity with which they picked up Urdu, English and Hindi. Hence, their lack of presence in the politics and bureaucracy in a united Andhra Pradesh or a newly formed Telangana.'

Through the Mulki agitation and the statehood movement in the 1950s and 1960s, English remained the more prestigious and useful language for pursuing an education. Telugu began to gain more importance from the 1970s onwards with the advent of NTR. 'English was necessary, but the 1970s and 1980s saw more prominence of Telugu,' Ravi Karan noted, 'I am perplexed as to why we did not incline our youth towards Telugu thirty years ago like we did with Persian, Urdu and Hindi.'

He then brought up an interesting question. 'What if a "son of the soil" movement emerges here?' Ravi Karan asked, perhaps alluding to frequent news from the neighbouring state of Karnataka, 'Kayasthas will stand to lose out on opportunities in business as well as the bureaucracy if we do not adopt Telugu. Thus, 70 to 80 per cent of qualified youngsters are now settled in the US, the UK and Canada due to the sense of belonging being very up and down here.'

Although it had been more than a few months since Narayan Raj Saxena died, when Karan spoke about this very real feeling of belonging, I immediately thought of the anonymous response from the younger Mathur Kayastha to which Bansi Raja's great-grandson took exception. Maybe this fluctuating sense of belonging that Dr Karan spoke of explains that youngster's response, which is quoted in the third edition of *Social History of an Indian Caste*.

Epilogue

1948 in 2024

In Krishan Chander's Urdu novel *Jab Khet Jaage*, there is a character called Maqbool, who is very obviously based on Makhdoom Mohiuddin. Maqbool is a trade unionist who exhorts factory workers in Hyderabad to stand up for themselves against exploitative employers. The protagonist is Raghu Rao, a landless peasant who moves to Hyderabad city from a rural Telangana district after being exploited by a landlord Jagan Nath Reddy.

Reddy's high-handedness is not limited to making Rao toil on his estate and palatial house. He goes so far as to have his way with the woman Rao loves, while forbidding him and his kin to enjoy the new clothes that they bought. To the landlord, a vetti (bonded labour) labourer can dress and carry himself like a vetti only.

When the plot moves to the city, there is a point where Rao asks Maqbool why Jagannath Reddy had called on the Razakars to suppress an uprising of his labourers. The battle had been bloody, in fiction as it was in real life. The Razakars were more than just accomplices in the bid of landlords to keep peasants and cultivators under their thumb. 'Profiteering and tyranny transcend religion,' Maqbool replies, 'It has always been the norm in the country for backward-thinking powers to fall back on communalism whenever they are on the wane.'[1]

Jab Khet Jaage was published in 1952, the year of India's first-ever general election. In the summer of 2024, as I was putting the finishing touches to this manuscript, India's eighteenth general election was underway. The ruling BJP hoped to cross 400 seats in the Lok Sabha but had to settle with 240. For the first time in a decade, they had to rely on allies to cobble together a majority to form a government. They had also just run the most communally charged campaign in recent times. On the campaign trail in Hyderabad, for instance, Home Minister Amit Shah had asked a gathering whether they would like to 'vote for jihad'—implying the Congress—or 'vote for development'.[2] The Bharatiya Rashtra Samithi was not spared either as he clubbed the Congress, BRS and MIM as a trifecta that indulged in 'appeasement politics'. I thought about how Maqbool's words are as relevant today in 2024 as they were in 1952.

In 2024, especially for an Indian Muslim, the political has become personal in a way that has made even living room chatter a minefield. Over the last few years, I have noticed many close acquaintances amplify revisionist histories in a manner that is insidious in its casualness. A particular incident comes to mind. In the summer of 2022, I happened to drop by an elderly family friend's house a day or two after an incident of communal violence in Delhi's Jahangirpuri area. According to reports, there had been stone-pelting at a procession taken for Hanuman Jayanti celebrations.

While we spoke, this friend showed me a cartoon that had been doing the rounds on WhatsApp. A doctor tells a Muslim patient—depicted with the stereotypical prayer cap—that he has a stone in his stomach. The patient responds: 'Leave it in there, it will be handy for the riots.' My friend was not in the least outraged or even resigned. He had shown me the image and guffawed, expecting me to find it funny and laugh with him.

This person who chuckled at that WhatsApp forward comes from a family that has a history of hobnobbing with the Muslim aristocracy. They have attended Muslim weddings, where they always relished the rich food and qawwali performances. Later, before I was leaving, my friend said in Dakhani, '*Agli baar tum aayinge na, main tum ku Nizam ke zamaane ke kuch kitaabaan de toon* (Next time you come by, I will give you some books from the Nizam era).'

Looking Beyond One's Own Backyard

Something has clearly shifted, as evidenced by the quote from the anonymous Kayastha youth in the 2020 edition of Karen Leonard's masterful study of the community. The young man spoke of the need to dissociate himself from the Asaf Jahi legacy of his forefathers because 'the Nizams inflicted a lot of pain on the Hindus of Telangana'.

The Muslim society of Hyderabad has come a long way since Police Action. It is visible in the city's real estate, educational, business and political landscapes. Minority institutions like Muffakham Jah College and Sultan-ul-Uloom College have helped many Muslims gain an engineering education that allowed them to compete for the jobs in HITEC city and abroad as well. The purchasing power for Hyderabad city's largest minority to buy land, send their kids to various educational institutions—both in Hyderabad and overseas—is to a great extent a result of the Saudi riyals and Emirati dinars earned in the Gulf.

But it is not only money that has come in from the Gulf. Since the 1990s, a Saudi-inspired hardline school of Islamic thought has made its presence felt in the city. More so in the diaspora, back in the 2000s, certain Hyderabadis felt that Arab clothes, cultures and customs (whose influences on the subcontinent cannot be overlooked of course) were superior to South Asian ones.

Aspects of the Gulf's cultural and religious practice have made their way to Hyderabad even as the economic reality in the region has changed rapidly. In Saudi Arabia especially, things are very different for Hyderabadi migrants, especially compared to the experience of the first few waves of migrations from the 1970s to the 1990s.

The indigenization that began in the 2000s has caught even more steam in the Kingdom during the last few years. There will come a time when mid-level jobs in small and medium enterprises and the retail sector will not be available to be filled by economic migrants from South Asia. One of the measures the Saudi government has brought in to encourage domestic employment is to increase the tax on non-nationals.

Even in the UAE, opportunities for Hyderabadi youth are shrinking. The country has introduced a Golden Visa, but that is mostly to encourage the ultra-wealthy to own property and have business interests in the country. Dubai may be becoming more of a paradise for the wealthy, but even white-collar workers are facing rising and unsustainable costs.[3]

My sense is that for the most part, Hyderabadi Muslims are yet to come to terms with this changing reality of the economic opportunity in the Gulf, specifically Saudi Arabia and the UAE. In a way, this wilful ignorance is reminiscent of the years leading up to Police Action. The Muslims of Hyderabad had turned a blind eye to the political and social movements that were taking place outside the Nizam's dominions. By the time they came to terms with the tide, it had already altered their lives completely.

Even city-dwelling Muslims have not been able to ignore the changed reality of the Indian Muslim. They cannot fully insulate themselves from the politics of hate and exclusion. In fact, because of its history and demographic, Hyderabad has always been sensitive to the slightest shift in communal relations. One of my motivations for writing this book was to challenge the narratives that present Asaf Jahi Hyderabad as a syncretic paradise, where Hindus and Muslims have always lived in immaculate harmony and collaboration. The forces that shaped much of the politics and public life in what is now the state of Telangana have always been communally tinged.

Isa-Moosi Tehzeeb

My other motivation for wanting to write this book was to bottle that amorphous thing that connects one Hyderabadi to another. Here, as often in the book, I use 'Hyderabadi' to mean anyone who has family ties to the vast region that once came under the princely state of Hyderabad. That thing is culture, an identity that goes beyond religion and race. It is a shared memory of food, language and geography, which is getting diluted with every generation, but still somehow survives in ways conscious and subconscious. It is what the Karachi-born Ali Adil Khan (Chapter 6) has in common with the communist-turned-educator Chukka Ramaiah (Chapter 7). It is what the statehood movement has been about, a contemporary avatar of the Mulki-non-Mulki debates that go back to the time of the Qutub Shahis.

Even when this 'thing' takes on a religious colour, it is meant to signify something composite, something that is unique in and of itself. The communist leader Burgula Narsing Rao, for instance, referred to it as Isa-Moosi tehzeeb, to distinguish it from the flavour of the Ganga-Jamuna tehzeeb, which is often used as shorthand to signify the composite culture and communal amity in the northern parts of the country. Rao's nomenclature is taken from the rivers of Hyderabad, once the lifelines of the city but which are now highly polluted.

The Ever-Evolving Hyderabad

The 'culture' exists in the collaborative spirit of the dwindling tribe of the city's journalists—people like Apparasu Srinivasa Rao (Chapter 8), Ayoob Ali Khan (Chapter 5), Serish Nanisetti, Yunus Lasania and Syed Mohammed, who are committed to chronicling

Hyderabad's glories and tragedies in a thorough manner. It exists at some Kayastha weddings where the red fez caps known as the Rumi topis are worn by guests. It exists in some Hyderabadi Muslim weddings, where the bride is made to wear the kalipot necklace called the mangalsutra in most parts of India.

The need to fly the nest is as much part of the Isa-Moosi tehzeeb as anything else. My father (Chapter 3), Mir Ayoob Ali Khan (Chapter 5) and numerous other Hyderabadis went to Saudi Arabia to build a life. Mohiuddin Qadri Zor and Abdul Qadir Sarwari (Chapter 4), too, left Hyderabad for Kashmir to spread the gospel of Urdu.

Many like Chukka Srinivas (Chapter 7), Sarwari's son, Vasiq, and Raj Bahadur Gour's grandsons (Chapter 9) were part of the wave of STEM graduates who left for the US and settled there.

The trajectory of Ali Adil Khan, his children and his parents spans three different countries. Abroad, Hyderabadis have created associations to stay in touch with their homeland. In the US and Canada, Telugu-speaking Hindus tend to gravitate towards regional and caste-based associations. Muslims have their own collectives, the gatherings of which mostly just entail women in khara dupattas and men in sherwanis enjoying qawwalis and/or rich Deccani cuisine.

While working on drafts of this book, I often found myself romanticizing the past and being alarmist about the present. Given my love for Urdu poetry, especially from Hyderabad, my tone also frequently slipped into elegy. These were also the modes of expression preferred by many of my protagonists, interlocutors and sources. But it slowly dawned on me (as I hope it has impressed itself on you) that these chapters are really about evolutions and how identities can shapeshift while remaining rooted in a chequered past. These identities challenge easily held assumptions and confront many inconvenient truths.

The thread that runs through each of the chapters is that their protagonists have all been touched by the events surrounding Police

Action and integration. From there, they shaped their destiny in interesting ways. Their stories, whether of an ordinary family man making a living in Saudi or a communist who had to go underground, convey something or the other that is essential about the Hyderabadi character—resilience, enterprise, quick wit and a penchant for nostalgia.

It is a nostalgia I often indulged because traces of the old Hyderabad are fast disappearing. One elderly person, who was born in the 1950s, once lamented to me that he saw Irani hotels being replaced by idli-dosa joints before his own eyes. In today's Hyderabad, which is the Indian outpost of some of the world's most well-known technology companies, even the idli-dosa joints are not as fashionable as the eateries serving Italian and Japanese cuisine. These newer joints now cater to the evolving tastes of its residents, many of whom arrive from different parts of India, not to advise the Nizam but to code and ship products in IT companies.

'*Baahir hotel mein khaana mu'ayyub samjha jata tha. Jis family ka ek bhi member baahir khaata tha, woh ghar mein shaadi ka rishta leke jaana ya aise ghar se rishte ki baat karna namumkin tha,*' the elder told me. (Eating at a restaurant was considered very improper. When parents used to look at prospective matches for a son or daughter, if even one member of that family was known to be someone who frequented restaurants, talk of marital reunion with their kith and kin was out of the question).

It is a time spoken of with great longing by older Muslim families. Whenever I venture to Paramount Colony in Toli Chowki to get my fix of cheap but authentic Middle Eastern food, my father reminds of how frowned upon it was to dine at a restaurant when he was growing up.

A More Contemporary Symbol of Isa-Moosi Tehzeeb

Yet, some aspects of the old Hyderabad remain, but presented in modern form. A few minutes from the Salar Jung Museum, which is a relic of the city's princely past, one can find shades of the pluralistic ethos of Hyderabad.

The House of Champions Mixed Martial Arts (MMA) Gym is no place for excuses or nawabi indolence as fighters hone their MMA skills under the rigorous tutelage of Shaik Khalid, a native of Yaqutpura in the Old City.[4]

Mahboob Khan, India's first gold medallist in the sport and professional MMA promotion aspirant, trained here along with Ramakrishna Allam, a native of Karimnagar.[5] Fighters from as far as Haryana and Uttar Pradesh come to train under Shaik Khalid.

Mahboob Khan himself is a symbol of Hyderabad's resilience after 1948. His great-grandfather had once been a police officer in Gulbarga and had narrowly escaped death during Police Action. He had on him a photograph of a Hindu deity, which had prevented the rioters from taking his life. He kept the photograph until his dying day. This ordeal had pushed Khan's grandfather into a life of poverty, from which the family only began to recover after moving to Hyderabad in 2007.

Though Shaik Khalid does not spend much time thinking about symbolism, his House of Champions Gym is one of the last bastions of Isa-Moosi tehzeeb. Under his roof, Muslim and Hindu fighters from various parts of Telangana and the country come together to train, spar and eat.

One can even consider House of Champions as a microcosm of Hyderabad's cosmopolitan nature. Prime Minister Jawaharlal Nehru alluded to this when he defined Hyderabad as a 'microcosm of Indian culture.'

Today, it is no surprise that Mercer's Quality of Living ranks Hyderabad as the best Indian city to live in.

The Urdu poet Firaq Gorakhpuri, who once hailed how various communities of the world had contributed to India being the mosaic of diverse cultures, languages, religions and customs, wrote the following about the country's sixth biggest metro city.

> *Hyderabad aah! Yek ek jannat-e-qalb-o-nigaah*
> *Haaye yeh andaz dil-kash haaye iss ka baankpan*[6]

> Oh Hyderabad! This paradise of the heart and sight
> Oh, its alluring and brazen ways

Hyderabadis have come a long way from Police Action to the present day. It is up to them to ensure that it remains an inclusive haven that people from all over India keep flocking to—especially in today's unique times.

Acknowledgements

The Hyderabadis had been almost five years in the making after I left Siasat.com.

As I went about turning this idea into the final product that you are holding in your hand, there are many whom have been of immense help in different ways—before, during and after I commenced the work on this book.

While the idea for *The Hyderabadis: From 1947 to the Present Day* was planted in Hyderabad's soil, only in Delhi could the concept move beyond the conceptual stage with the help of a more robust publishing ecosystem. Thus, first and foremost, it is only right that I begin thanking people from the city which poets like Mirza Ghalib, Mir Taqi Mir and Mohammed Ibrahim Zauq called home.

Aditya Sinha, RT's India features editor, is a generous soul for whom I have also have had the fortune of writing a piece on a renowned communist from Pakistan whose roots lay in Hyderabad. When I met him for the first time in late 2021—thanks to an introduction by poet and English literature professor Ashley Tellis—I told Aditya about my idea for this book. I mentioned that I had already began research interviews but that the process of approaching agents and publishers seemed daunting.

In less than twenty-four hours, he made an introduction to Kanishka Gupta, the prolific agent of Writer's Side. The next day, when I got a call from Kanishka at the household of dear family friends, the Sawhneys-Suris, I was heartened that a seasoned publishing veteran believed in my idea. One of his team members, Narayani Basu, helped me put together a proposal based off on some interviews and early research that I had undertaken.

Kanishka diligently went about procuring a deal, but Amarjit Singh Dulat, too, was helpful during this phase.

Swati Chopra, who was then associated with HarperCollins India, was quick to also see potential in my idea and make an offer.

All these aforementioned Delhi NCR folks have played a role in enabling my entry into the world that seemed so intimidating a few years ago. Their help means a lot!

I have also been fortunate to have certain guiding hands during the past decade who provided some direction as I went about pursuing different feature stories pertaining to South Asia. Back in 2016, Raza Rumi was the first person who encouraged me to write for outlets in Pakistan. Three years later, Mir Ayoob Ali Khan helped me really understand Hyderabad and its people, both before and after my Siasat.com tenure. Not too long after I left Siasat.com to start interviewing and researching for *The Hyderabadis*, I realized that there were plenty of Urdu-centric stories that had been brewing in my mind for quite some time. Nipa Charaghi asked me to pitch them to *Mint Lounge*, a publication for which she serves as deputy editor.

Learning how to read and write the nastaleeq script enabled me to write these stories from a more substantive, insider lens, rather than using an exotic gaze. I owe this ability to proficiently read and write the script to two people—the late Khalid Saeed of MANUU and Naresh Sharma, my Urdu literacy instructor at SOAS. The former gave me his workbook that enabled to me to learn the letters and write basic sentences. The latter was a fun instructor who helped me become more proficient with my Urdu reading and writing.

Be it a certain push in the right direction, the right advice at the right time, a workbook, a platform, or even the smallest piece of historical knowledge, I am grateful to all of these people who have been guiding hands.

~

Whether it was improving my spoken Urdu during my MA in London or my numerous trips to MANUU in Hyderabad, my experiences of learning the language and its literature—both in and outside of a classroom—have been nothing short of enlightening due to the following people.

My friends from the across the border—Hammad, Hassan, Ayesha and Shah ji—were the first people with whom I could really practice my advanced spoken Urdu.

Back in Hyderabad, outside the enriching yet fragmented Urdu circles, these immersive environments where I could use and learn Urdu vocabulary were few and far between. But thanks to certain MANUU students and friends, specifically those from Jammu and Kashmir (Attaullah Niazi, Ahjaz Chaudhry, Liaquat Chaudhry, Maqbool Bhatti, Tehwer Iqbal and Tajammul Islam), I could keep learning and utilizing my Urdu vocabulary. Niazi was also the one who formally introduced me to Umar Faruq Quadri (Chapter 2).

~

Dr Amena Tehseen and Professor Kalaam are two people at MANUU with whom interviews and casual discussions provided a lot of the context for some reportage that fed into this book. Although now retired, Professor Naseemuddin Farees, who is an authority on Dakhani, is another stalwart from MANUU. Long conversations with Shams Imran, whom one can find at the university's Directorate of Distance Education, have helped shape how I view and analyse trends of the past, present and future.

~

Though I can only nurture these intellectual pursuits due to my mother Rubina, father Majid (Chapter 3) and sister Beesyna. Their support is the main reason I am able to do this. It has been quite the journey that has spanned four different countries with them. Their love and support throughout the ups and downs is why I am able to find and tell certain stories that I am passionate about.

My extended family in the West, two hours away from Toronto and about thirty minutes outside Washington DC, have also been among my biggest cheerleaders ever since they heard the news of my book deal. Certain family members back in Hyderabad have also played the same role.

One of them, whom I would like to mention, is Maqsood Mamu. Being a true-blue Old City wala, it is because of him that I discovered the gold mines of literary and historical Urdu books in Mahub Chowk nearby. Without his help, I would have never found out that Chowk was home to these stores that contained Urdu as well as English gems—many of which are listed in the bibliography.

~

Hanaan and Mohammed at Chowk's Islamic Book Depot, where I found the extremely rare collections of Wajida Tabassum, are always helpful. At Maqbool Book Depot, I came upon Krishan Chander's reportage of his trip to Nizam-era Hyderabad for the Progressive Writers' Association Conference. Ghouse Pasha is so warm and welcoming whenever I visit Maqbool Depot.

The Bafanas, who owned and operated Haziq & Mohi, have also been accessible. Although in Delhi, Bahrisons in Khan Market and Midland Book Shop in Hauz Khas are places that have been literary havens for me outside Hyderabad. Shafiq at Bahrisons went all out in finding a Partition-centric book that my agent asked me to read as it was similar to the idea for *The Hyderabadis*. The Baig family, who own Midland, always provide the flavour of the Deccan up in Delhi at their outlets.

Aside from bookstores and the helping hands there, there were those who either gifted or let me borrow some important primary and secondary sources that were integral in helping me build the worlds and eras from 1948–2024. I owe my gratitude to many such people for not only indirectly adding more works to my bookshelves, but apprising me of some very valuable sources.

Moses Tulasi let me borrow and copy Venkateswara Rao Adiraju's *Telangana: Saga of a Tragic Struggle*. Dr Rafiuddin Farouqui lent me his compilation of Syed Abul Ala Maududi's letters, one in which the Jamaat-e-Islami founder attempts to convince Qasim Razvi into forgetting the pipe dream of an independent Hyderabad. Sarah Waheed was kind enough to send her scholarly article that was published by *Asian Affairs*.

Praveen Balaji's self-published interview of his grandfather Raj Bahadur Gour (Chapter 9) that Tamara Gour gave me is nothing less than a treasure. Another treasure is the tribute which Ali Adil Khan put together for his father Anwar Ali (Chapter 6). Even with Gour and Ali having left for their heavenly abodes, these self-published sources also enabled me to see history through the eyes of those who are no longer with us.

Leftist activist Burgula Narsing Rao's compilation of interviews and writings titled *Living Those Times* is an encompassing work. It captures different layers (especially with respect to the Telangana Rebellion) of Police Action. The second time I met Rao's son, Vijay, and told him about my project, he instantly gave me a copy of *Living Those Times*. This was one of many early works through which I learned about the Telangana Rebellion. Had it not been for K. Srinivas, an editor of the regional newspaper *Andhra Jyothi*, who is also an erudite scholar of Telugu literature that pertains to the Telangana Armed Struggle, I would not have known of Devulapalli Venkateshwara Rao's *Telangana Prajala Sayudha Porata Charitra*, which contained the story of Sheikh Bandagi.

Ibrahim Jalees' evocative memoir from which I recreated the interaction between him, the Progressive-turned-Razakar, and Gour was gifted to me by Tarun Pant, an ardent Gurgaon-based Urduphile. We had first interacted when he reached out enquiring about the contact information of the owners of some Chowk book depots after reading a piece I had authored for *Mint Lounge*.

Be it *Lounge* or other publications like *Hindu Business Line's Ink* or *The News Minute*, Aditi Sengupta, Samiksha Bharadwaj and Vidya Sigamani were some editors whose feedback for many Hyderabad-centric pieces made me think differently about historical events and other aspects of the city's heritage differently.

It was during my one-year tenure at Siasat.com where the original idea for this book materialized. But even after I left, the office continued to be a workspace for me. Just a week or two after leaving the company, Zaheer Ali Khan was the very first one to speak to me about Abid Ali Khan (Chapter 1). He and his son, Asghar, who also handles the IT, were always supportive of this project and my two mini documentaries.

Minhaj Adnan, Abdullahi 'Aboudi' Abdulrahman and Siddhant Thakur were both excellent editors and cameramen as I began dabbling in documentary film-making. The coffees, chai and green teas made by Azhar and Ahmed bhai were also very replenishing. Harsha Panyam was such a sport when it came to proofreading early drafts of two chapters. He also orally translated a chapter about Sheikh Bandagi's story from Devulapalli Venkateshwara Rao's *Telangana Prajala Sayudha Porata Charitra* for me.

~

When Sruthi Apparasu also worked at Siasat.com, she put me in touch with her father ASR (Chapter 8). Not only did he tell me plenty about the Telangana struggle as a journalist but also as someone who cast his lot for a separate state. Though I do remember the lead-up to the state formation in 2013, I did not see much of the struggle play out when the statehood push resurfaced in 2009 as I had not been living in Hyderabad.

ASR spared time to speak with me about the fight for Telangana. He then kindly agreed to converse with me about his own family. I could not be more thankful to him and the Hyderabadis featured in all ten chapters as they were gateways to various eras of the city's history from Police Action to more recent times.

Although he was not someone whose family I chronicled, my dear friend Nikhil's father Gopal Dasari, too, told me some interesting background information about the 1969 agitation. He had witnessed the first push for a state in 1969 as a student. Gopal Garu also attuned me to how the Kothagudem debacle was one of the major sparks for turning the disenchantment among Telanganites into a full-fledged demand for bifurcation.

Well-known journalist and author Serish Nanisetti openly spoke to me of his early interactions with Ayoob Ali Khan (Chapter 5) from their *Deccan Chronicle* days.

Thank you all very much for opening up your homes and workplaces to me to patiently answer a lot of follow-up questions during various rounds of edits.

~

Oudesh Rani Bawa has always been a grandmother-like treasure trove of knowledge ever since I began writing about Hyderabad. City historian and family friend Sajjad Shahid is another approachable person who is always willing to share whatever he knows about the Deccan. For numerous clarifications about certain events in history during the editing stage, especially pertaining to Osmania University and Urdu, I would call *Shugoofa* magazine's chief editor Mustafa Kamal. He, too, was responsive and helped me with a lot of my questions.

The late Rahim Khan, who once served as secretary of Urdu Hall in Himayat Nagar, is someone who always invited me to his office whenever there was a book, paper or any point of contact that he thought would be of help. That too, regardless of whether he knew what I was working on. Even before I got a book deal, he made a copy of Akhtar Hassan's old *Sab-Ras* article for me. That was particularly useful for Abid Ali Khan's chapter. About two or three weeks before HarperCollins India made an offer, he passed away. It was also due to him I got be acquainted with the last six authentic versifiers among a dying breed of Dakhani humour poets: Moin Amar 'Bamboo', Shahed Adeeli, Lateefuddin Lateef, Fareed Saher, Chicha Palmoory and Waheed Pasha Quadri. If I was able to get a taste of the Dakhani Mazahiya Shayari that helped many Hyderabadis emerge from the tragedy of Police Action, it is because of these funny men.

~

I surely would not have come to know about Hyderabad's Urdu luminaries Mohiuddin Qadri Zor and Abdul Qadir Sarwari (even though the latter's son turned out to be a family friend and the former was acquainted with my maternal side of the family in Kashmir) if it was not for Zamir Ahmad Butt. Only at an event about a Kashmir-centric anthology-cum-photobook at HITEC City in 2018, did I learn about those two Urdu legends. While conversing with the anthology's editor and letting him know that my maternal family lived in the Valley from the mid-1950s till the militancy phase, I am glad that Zamir, then a PhD candidate at the University of Hyderabad and a Srinagar native, happened to be listening to that conversation. He suggested right away that we write something about Hyderabadis who lived in Kashmir from the 1950s to the 1990s. I readily agreed with the idea.

The result is a full-fledged chapter and a tribute to two towering figures of Urdu in Hyderabad.

A few others who currently live in Kashmir helped out with introductions to Kashmiri litterateurs who were lucky enough to be Baba-e-Deccaniyat's and Imam-e-Urdu's students.

During a trip to Srinagar in the summer of 2022, I had walked into the University of Kashmir's Urdu department on a whim. A friendly PhD candidate there at that time, Irfan Rasheed, introduced me to Dr Mushtaq Haider and Dr Aijazuddin Shaikh. They had told me about some of Zor and Sarwari's students who went on to do great things. Conversations with them were possible due to Haider and Shaikh putting Zamir and me in touch with them.

Of course, books and existing contacts can get one off to a great start when researching, interviewing and writing. But getting introduced to new people whom I was not acquainted with earlier is what really allowed me to have a more diverse range of families, layers and angles through which I could chronicle different phases of Hyderabad's contemporary history.

There were those who were more than willing to make introductions. The different individuals they introduced me to often informed me about relevant books that came in handy for research and suggested that I speak to their acquaintances, whose families have had interesting trajectories since 1948. Hyderabad Urban Lab's Anant Maringanti and Toronto-based Meenakshi Alimchandani connected me to Chukka Srinivas (Chapter 7) and Ali Adil Khan respectively. I am also very fortunate that Anoop Raj Saxena referred me to Bansi Raja's great-grandson (Chapter 10).

Yunus 'That Hyderabadi Boy' Lasania directed me towards Vijay Burgula. When carrying out further research for the second chapter, Syed Ghiyasuddin readily referred me to Rafiudduin Farouqui.

~

I would like to mention other friends and acquaintances who are in different parts of the world.

Oddly enough, sometimes a visit to Shaik Khalid's Hyderabad MMA gym on Kali Khabar Road in Old City helped to get my creative juices flowing. May he and his assistant coach Bilal keep churning out fighters who give the rest of the country's fighters some tough competition and do Hyderabad proud!

Ruzbeh Hodiwala and Kunal Purohit (who has written the wonderful yet harrowing *H-Pop*) are two friends from my SOAS days who have been well-wishers during and after grad school.

Ahmed Baig cooked some excellent food for Ali Adil Khan and me at the Brampton location of his restaurant Baig's Grill as we conversed about Adil's family's trajectory that spanned India, Pakistan and Canada. Not only is Ahmed a great chef, but an author in the making as well. I cannot wait for his book on the history of kababs to come out!

South of the border, Zach Flum, Brian Kingan, Eric Polanco and Hari Prasad are some buddies who have been my genuine supporters from afar.

In central New Jersey, management professor Raza Mir has done nothing but encourage my endeavours to dig out nuggets about

Hyderabad's history ever since we were introduced by a mutual Toronto-based acquaintance. He is also the author of three excellent books. One of these works is a historical fiction novel, while the other two are primers on Mirza Ghalib and Allama Iqbal. I could not be luckier to have a foreword penned by Mir.

~

Lastly, I would like to end this lengthy vote of thanks with the name of one person without whom *The Hyderabadis* would not have taken the shape it finally did. Vikram Shah has edited a lot of excellent stories for *Mint Lounge* and the (unfortunately) discontinued online long-form publication *Fifty-Two*. His meticulous inputs were of immense help.

Thank you very much Vikram for helping me turning this book into the best version of itself!

Notes

Scan this QR code to access the detailed notes.

Index

About the Author

Daneesh Majid is a Hyderabad-based writer who concentrates on South Asian culture, security and Urdu literature. He has worked for Siasat.com, the online English edition of the prominent Urdu daily. His writing has been featured in numerous South Asian media outlets, such as *Mint Lounge*, *The Hindu Business Line*, *Express Tribune*, *The New Indian Express*, The Wire, The News Minute, ThePrint, Madras Courier, DailyO, *The Nation* (Pakistan) and *Dhaka Tribune*. He is an alumnus of Franklin and Marshall College, Pennsylvania, and the School of Oriental and African Studies (SOAS), University of London.